Children of Six Cultures

Children of Six Cultures
A Psycho-Cultural Analysis

Beatrice B. Whiting and John W. M. Whiting
in Collaboration with Richard Longabaugh

Based on Data Collected by
John and Ann Fischer
Robert LeVine and Barbara Lloyd
Thomas and Hatsumi Maretzki
Leigh Minturn
William and Corinne Nydegger
A. Kimball and Romaine Romney

Harvard University Press
Cambridge, Massachusetts, and London, England

To Our Junior Colleagues
in Palfrey House, 1955–1962,
and William James Hall, 1962–1972

Preface

This book, the most recent report of the Six Culture Study, aims to add to our knowledge of the varieties of social behavior of children brought up in different parts of the world. Earlier research on comparative child development (Whiting and Child, 1953) indicated that such an approach was promising but that more standardized procedures for collecting data were required. The diversity of the practices reported in ethnographic literature showed how restricted and parochial were the descriptions of methods of child care and training characteristic of the cultures of modern Western societies. Although available reports written by anthropologists, missionaries, and colonial administrators were usually scant when it came to children, there was enough material to indicate wide variations in the nature of the social and physical environment that individuals of different cultures experienced from birth to adulthood.

The hypotheses the Whiting and Child study set out to test were derived from the Freudian assumption that experiences during infancy and childhood had an effect on adult personality. Some of these hypotheses were confirmed but many were not. This made the inadequate and unsystematic reporting of the early ethnographies especially frustrating. We did not know whether to attribute our failures to false assumptions or inadequate data. We therefore decided that an attempt should be made to collect systematic data on child life in a variety of cultures.

To accomplish this aim the Committee on Social Behavior of the Social Science Research Council, of which Robert Sears was Chairman, was persuaded to sponsor a seminar and a conference on the cross-cultural study of socialization. This resulted in the development of a plan (Whiting et al., 1953) which eventuated in the Six Culture Study.* Irvin L. Child, William W. Lambert and John W. M. Whiting were principle investigators and Beatrice B. Whiting the coordinator of the study. The field research was carried out by six teams: John and Ann Fischer; Robert LeVine and Barbara LeVine [Lloyd]; Thomas and Hatsumi Maretzki; Leigh Minturn; William and Corinne Nydegger; and A. Kimball and Romaine Romney. The field teams were assisted by graduates of local universities and schools: Nariyuki Agarie, Gurdeep Jaspal, Simeon Nyashai, John Okiamba, Felix Ombasa, Laurence Sagini, Sri Shyam Narain Singh, Taurino Singson, Muriel Eva Verbitsky and Kiyoshi Yogi.

The research plan was developed collaboratively by the field teams and the principle investigators during a six-week session just prior to the beginning of the fieldwork. The plan produced during this

*Robert Sears, Pauline Sears, Eleanor Maccoby, and Barbara Ayres were especially helpful in developing the plan. A generous grant from the Behavioral Science Division of the Ford Foundation made it possible to carry it out. The fieldwork and part of the analysis and writing of five of the six reports were financed by this grant. Later analysis and editing were supported by a grant from the United States Public Health Service.

[handwritten: ethnography. The scientific description of the cultures and customs of various nations or peoples]

session, together with comments and criticisms written during and after the fieldwork, constitutes one of the publications resulting from the project (Whiting et al., 1965).

[handwritten: Each team was responsible for:]

Each field team was responsible for writing a general ethnography of the community under study, as well as a detailed description of child-rearing and child life at the cultural level. These were published in a single volume (B. Whiting, 1963), and separately, in paperback form.* *[handwritten: (1) (2) (3)]*

The plan also called for the field teams to draw a sample of children and give standard interviews to their mothers. These interviews were analyzed and the results written up by Minturn and Lambert (1964). Finally, each field team, together with its research assistants, was expected to collect a large number of standard observations of the behavior of the children of the sample in natural settings. The analysis of these data is the subject of this monograph.

Many individuals have worked on the coding and analysis of the data over the past years. The roster includes the staff and students of the Laboratory of Human Development, Harvard University, from 1954 to 1962, particularly Richard Longabaugh, Thomas Landauer, A. Kimball Romney, Roy D'Andrade, Sadako Imamura, Mark Weisman, and Jean Altman. From 1962 to 1972 the staff and students of the Social Relations department contributed their time and energy, particularly Mary Lou Lionells and Michael Burton, who worked as postdoctoral fellows; Charles Harrington, Gary Granz-

---

*Published by John Wiley and Sons, New York, in 1964, the individual monographs are: Fischer and Fischer, *The New Englanders of Orchard Town;* LeVine and LeVine [Lloyd], *Nyansongo: A Guisii Community in Nyansongo;* Maretzki and Maretzki, *Taira: An Okinawan Village;* Minturn and Hitchcock, *The Rajputs of Khalapur;* Nydegger and Nydegger, *Tarong: An Ilocos Barrio in the Philippines;* Romney and Romney, *The Mixtecans of Juxtlahuaca, Mexico.*

berg, and Lawrence Baldwin, graduate students; and Mary MacCrea, Bonnie Grey, and Wendy Jackson, research assistants.

Throughout the years the person who has contributed most consistently is Richard Longabaugh. His analysis of the interrelation of the behaviors selected for study has appeared in two publications, *A Category System for Coding Interpersonal Behavior as Social Exchange* (1963), and *The Structure of Interpersonal Behavior* (1966).

William Lambert of Cornell has worked on the analysis of aggressive behavior. His results will be published in a separate volume.

At times, the data seemed insurmountable. Certainly the present volume would be very different had it not been for the development of computer programs suitable for the analysis of social science data. We have grown up with these programs and have benefited by them. The staff and students involved in the analysis profited in countless ways which cannot be measured by this volume. Stimulated by working on the project, they have increased their knowledge of the problems of cross-cultural research and have developed new methods and techniques for recording, coding, and comparing behavior observed in diverse natural settings. Some former staff and students have—perhaps because of the many years consumed in the analysis—been permanently discouraged from using behavior measures based on naturalistic observations. We hope that this volume will not only hearten those who are committed to such research but convince others that the problems of analysis are not insurmountable.

April 1974

Beatrice Whiting

John W. M. Whiting

Contents

Figures

Tables

Tables

Children of Six Cultures

ENVIRONMENT
- Climate
- Flora (plant)
- Fauna (animal)
- Terrain

HISTORY
- Migrations
- Borrowings
- Inventions

MAINTENANCE SYSTEMS
- Subsistence patterns
- Means of production
- Settlement patterns
- Social structure
- Systems of defense
- Law and social control
- Division of labor

CHILD'S LEARNING ENVIRONMENT
- Settings occupied
- Caretakers and teachers
- Tasks assigned
- Mother's workload

THE INDIVIDUAL ADULT

LEARNED:
- Behavioral styles
- Skills and abilities
- Value priorities
- Conflicts
- Defenses

INNATE:
- Needs
- Drives
- Capacities

INFANT

PROJECTIVE-EXPRESSIVE SYSTEMS
- Religion
- Magic beliefs
- Ritual and ceremony
- Art and recreation
- Games and play
- Crime rates
- Suicide rates

A Model for Psycho-Cultural Research.

(heuristic model)

1   Introduction

Are children brought up in societies with different customs, beliefs, and values radically different from each other? Do differences attributable to sex, age, and birth order override these cultural differences? Does the situation and setting influence a child's behavior or are his actions similar across environments? Or, to ask these questions in a summary form, if you want to predict the behavior of a preadolescent child, which would it be most important to know: his or her sex, age, birth order, the culture into which he was born or the situation he was in at the moment you made your prediction. Our study attempts to answer these questions by analyzing in natural settings and in the normal course of living the social behavior of a sample of boys and girls, three to eleven years of age, growing up in six different parts of the world.

Until recently, most research in child development has been concerned with differences among samples of individual children from the same culture. The effects of sex, age, birth order, and the child-rearing practices of the mother usually have been selected as the variables presumed to affect the abilities, personality, and behavior of the child. Except for some early cross-cultural research and more recent studies of cognitive development in other societies, culture as a variable has been used implicitly rather than explicitly. Many studies have shown differences between social classes or between ethnic groups,* but the meaning of the differences in terms of cultural values was rarely explored systematically. Studies reporting, for example, that lower-class parents are more likely to use physical rather than psychological techniques of punishment generally left it at that and did not question why this should be so, or whether the same difference would be expected in other cultures with social class systems.

When culture has been taken as a variable to be studied, the beliefs, values, and techniques of a whole society, or at least of the members of a band or hamlet or village, have been given unitary values as though everyone in the group accepted them. Variations of individuals within the society have been wiped out on the assumption that custom compels consensus.

In our Six Culture Project we tried to combine cross-cultural and intracultural approaches. The same children were compared with other children within their culture as well as those of different cultures. It must be admitted that with but six cultures and sixteen to twenty-four boys and girls varying from three to eleven years in age

---

*Early cross-cultural studies are those of Kardiner, 1939, 1945; Erikson, 1939, 1950; Whiting and Child, 1953; Barry, Bacon, and Child, 1957, 1959. Examples of recent cross-cultural studies in cognitive development are Bruner et al., 1966; Dawson, 1967; Goodnow, 1967; Price-Williams, 1969; Cole, 1971; and Dasen, 1973. For reviews see LeVine, 1970; Dasen, 1972. Studies of differences between social classes or ethnic groups are reviewed by Hess, 1970.

for our intracultural tests, we had the barest minimum of cases to test our hypotheses. To obtain significant differences, relations between variables had to be both strong and consistent. On the other hand, with such small sample sizes little confidence can be placed on the failure of the data to support a hypothesized relation. In other words, the study is particularly vulnerable to what statisticians refer to as "type-two error." Despite this defect, the opportunity of a six-fold replication of intracultural hypotheses and the opportunity of testing the same hypothesis both within and across cultures is a powerful feature of the design and makes up to some degree for the inadequacy resulting from small sample size.

Another important purpose of our study is the investigation of the transcultural validity of findings of studies on children in Europe and the United States. Most child psychologists have implicitly assumed that the effects of sibling order or the differences between boys and girls are universally true, although, when challenged, they will admit that their sample by no means represents the universe of all children from all cultures. The assumption made by some anthropologists that the children of each culture develop in a unique manner is equally fallacious. Again, assumptions of universality or uniqueness must be investigated, and an attempt will be made to test the generality of a limited set of hypotheses for six different cultures. Although the cultures of our study by no means represent the universe, such replication is a small step toward a test of universality.

The formulation of hypotheses for this project was guided by a set of underlying assumptions about the direction of causation in social change. This can be expressed in a heuristic model that begins with the environment and history and ends with religion and ideology;

heuristic
↓
serving to
find out
or discover.

this has been discussed in detail elsewhere.* Here we will be dealing with only that part of the model which takes the maintenance systems of a culture as a starting point. These systems include subsistence patterns, means of production, division of labor, social structure, settlement patterns, and systems of defense, law, and social control. The maintenance systems are assumed to determine to a large extent the learning environment in which the child grows up. His play space and playmates, his caretakers, his teachers, the tasks that he is assigned, the workload of his mother, his opportunity to interact with his father are all compellingly influenced by them. It is this learning environment that has the strongest influence upon the social behavior of the child.

The choice of the type of dependent variable to focus on posed a problem. Some of the measures used in earlier culture and personality research—magico-religious beliefs (Linton and Kardiner, 1939), folk tales (McClelland, 1952), magical theories of disease (Whiting and Child, 1953)—were inappropriate because they were conceptualized at the cultural level and could not be used to measure differences between individual children within a culture. Most of the studies that tested samples of individuals in other cultures had used the Rorschach test on the grounds that it was "culture free" (Hallowell, 1942; DuBois, 1944; Wallace, 1952; Gladwin and Sarason, 1953; Spindler, 1955). Its doubtful validity, when used by psychologists in our own culture (Dollard, 1953; Zubin, 1954), led us to reject it. The Thematic Apperception Test had also been used in other cultures (for review

*This model has been described in detail in Whiting, 1973. Previous research by the authors dealt with different parts of the model: the effects of environment on maintenance systems (Whiting, 1968); of history on maintenance systems (Whiting et al., 1966); and of the child's learning environment on projective-expressive systems (Whiting and Child, 1953; B. Whiting, 1965).

4

see Henry, 1956; Kaplan, 1961), most recently only after the pictures had been redrawn which made comparison difficult. Doll play, a projective test designed for younger children (P. Sears, 1948), was rejected on the grounds that it might not be appropriate in cultures where children do not play with dolls. Furthermore, the conclusions of all these projective tests were highly inferential. Child psychologists reported that interviews were not very successful with children under seven; since we wanted an instrument that could be used on younger as well as older children, we rejected this as our primary instrument.

There was a precedent for using behavior as a measure of personality in culture and personality studies. Margaret Mead (1935) had used the feminine and hypermasculine behavior of men as an index of temperament. Ruth Benedict (1934) had used Appolonian and Dionysian behavior to characterize patterning at the cultural level. And Eric Erikson (1939) used the warlikeness of the Pine Ridge Sioux as an index of a feature of their personality. Although a sample of individuals were not systematically observed in these studies, they did indicate that behavior could be used as an index of personality.

Although no observational study of the behavior of individual children in non-Western cultures had been attempted, research in our own culture (Sears et al., 1953; Beller, 1953; Gewirtz, 1954; Koch, 1955; Barker and Wright, 1954) suggested that it would be feasible, and we chose this as the method for measuring our dependent variable. Two other decisions had to be made: should we observe children in natural settings, and should we attempt to observe and record all acts or only a restricted range? The first decision was comparatively easy. To contrive an experimental setting for observation which would be comparable across the six cultures was not feasible without

5

considerably more foreknowledge of the cultures; even then it would be, we felt, a dubious procedure. The work of Barker and Wright (1954) indicated that, although observing children in natural settings was very costly in time and effort (and it turned out to be so in this study), it could be done with reasonable reliability.

The question as to whether we should restrict the range of behavior to be observed was more difficult, but we decided to do so for the following reasons. First, in pretests carried on during the year before going into the field it was discovered that there was very little agreement between the reports of two observers who were instructed to observe everything a child did, whereas with practice the agreement was acceptable if they were instructed to focus their attention solely on the child's interaction with other children and adults. Second, the nonsocial behavior of children, particularly fantasy and autistic behavior, was, like projective tests, difficult to interpret, whereas social behavior had a face validity that seemed more practical for the purposes of our study. The social behavior of children was therefore chosen as the domain for the dependent variables of the study, and standardized observations in natural settings as our method. The variables and the methods of observing, recording, and analyzing will be described in Chapter 3.

Referring again to our heuristic model, it is evident that each link in the chain of causal implications requires a distinct set of hypotheses. For the relation of environment and history to maintenance systems one would draw upon theories of cultural evolution. Erikson and Piaget would be fruitful sources of hypotheses for the motivational and cognitive developmental shifts from childhood to adulthood. Freudian theory is a useful source of hypotheses for predicting the relation between a child's learning environment and measures of adult personality.

A different set of assumptions are required for the present inquiry. Comparative ethnography, which has specified the features necessary to describe the varieties of subsistence types, social and political organizations, family types, settlement patterns, and household arrangements, is an invaluable source for isolating and defining the variables that link maintenance systems to the child's learning environment. A functional theory of the Malinowskian type is a useful source of hypotheses relevant to this link.

A number of theories were drawn upon to formulate hypotheses about the linkage between learning environments and social behavior. Most important of these is learning theory as formulated by Hull (1943) and Miller and Dollard (1941). Specifically, we assumed, first, that behavior is activated by drives that may be innate, such as hunger, thirst, or pain. Our second assumption was that the specific responses a child will make in a given situation, when activated by a drive, will be determined by experiences that the child previously had in that situation. A response that has previously led to the reduction of a drive (reward) will be more likely to occur than one that has failed to do so. Drive reduction is referred to as reinforcement; the failure of drive reduction is referred to as extinction. We assumed next that punishment (pain induction) has the effect of inducing the child to avoid or escape from a situation. This differs from the assumption made by other learning theories (Skinner, 1938; Pavlov, 1927) that punishment is simply negative reinforcement. Fourth, responses which are sometimes but not always successful lead to an increase in the state of drive (activation of the adrenal cortex due to uncertainty) and hence an increased amplitude of whatever response may occur. Our final assumption was that similar situations tend to evoke similar responses and the probability of a response occurring is a function of the similarity of the situations. Thus, a child who has been reinforced by being nurturant to a younger sibling is likely to be nurturant to other young children.

We also borrowed two important assumptions from social learning theory. The first is that reinforcement may be either extrinsic—such as rewards, non-rewards, and punishment administered by socializing agents—or intrinsic—that is, inherent in the nature of the act performed (Child, 1954). To hear an infant crying is unpleasant. Thus, a caretaker who stops her charge from crying by comforting the baby will be intrinsically rewarded for this behavior. She need not be praised by her parents to learn how to comfort crying infants. The second assumption is that children will identify with and imitate the behavior of their socializing agents. The degree to which this occurs is assumed to vary with the salience of the socializing agent, and the child's perception of the power of the agent, that is, the agent's control over resources, goods, privileges, and services desired by the child (Whiting, 1960). In most cultures the mother of an infant is perceived as being both most salient and most powerful and hence the prime candidate for identification and imitation. The salience and power of the father, *as perceived by the child*, varies markedly from culture to culture (Burton and Whiting, 1961).

The above hypotheses were not formulated precisely enough to enable us to go to the field with a set of theorems to test. They did, however, enable us to outline our general expectations; these are stated in the *Field Guide for a Study of Socialization* (Whiting et al., 1966). In this monograph we made no attempt to follow these predictions, nor did we attempt systematically to test the implications of the theories outlined above. Rather, we used the theory as a basis ← *Note* for the strategies chosen for data collection and data analysis and to interpret and elucidate our findings. Which assumptions turned out to be the most valid and useful will be reported in Chapter 9.

Finally, earlier library research and the results obtained from analysis of the interviews with the mothers of the sample children (Minturn and Lambert, 1964) concerning the effect of the maintenance systems and social structure upon child-training practices led us whenever possible to examine our data in the light of these findings. However, since in none of these studies was the behavior of children the dependent variable, the bearing of our findings on previous research is highly inferential. The hypotheses supported by previous cross-cultural research are as follows (1) Children raised in polygynous households, or households where the men do not sleep with their wives, have little contact with their fathers during the first two years of life, perceive their mother as the controller of resources, and identify with her. If they live in a society with strong patrilineal bias and male dominance, as young boys they will be in conflict over their sex identity and will be more aggressive to express their "protest masculinity." In contrast, in monogamous nuclear families, where the father is intimately involved in the domestic life, young boys will identify with their fathers at an early age and have less need to be aggressive (Burton and Whiting, 1961; B. Whiting, 1965) (2) Children raised in households in which the mother has few economic or ceremonial duties will not be subjected to socialization pressures at such a young age as those growing up in a household where the mother has many such duties. It was predicted that the former group as adults would be more trusting of others and more sociable (Whiting et al.,

recall from L.

1966), but the specifics of the expected behavior of three- to ten-year-olds were not detailed. (3) Children raised in extended families or in families which included two adult females would be treated with more indulgence in infancy (Murdock and Whiting, 1951). (4) Children brought up in societies with property such as livestock and surplus produce would be expected to be more obedient and more responsible than children raised in societies with low accumulation of property (Barry, Child, and Bacon, 1959). (5) Children raised in extended family households would be more severely punished for aggression than children raised in monogamous nuclear families (Whiting et al., 1966).

interesting

interesting

The dependent variables in this study are based on the social behavior of children observed in natural settings. The independent variables consist of the type of learning environment provided by the culture in which the child is brought up; the sex of the child; the age of the child; the nature of the situation in which the child is being observed; and differences in the learning environments within a culture that distinguish some individual children from others. We assume that each of these five factors has an independent effect, but we make no prior judgment as to which has the greatest influence.

A The dependent variables in this study are based on the social behavior of children observed in natural settings.

The [independent variables consist of:

① type of learning environ. provided by the culture in which the child is brought up

② sex of child
③ age of child
④ nature of the sit. in which the child is being observed
⑤ diffs. in the learning environs. within a culture that distinguish some individual children from others.

2   Setting and Sample

With the exception of those in Orchard Town, all the families in our study were predominately subsistence farmers.* Beginning with the Pacific, Thomas and Hatsumi Maretzki's community of Taira was located on the northeast coast of Okinawa, largest of the southern-most islands of the Ruyukyu chain. The central village where the children lived borders on the Bay of Taira, bounded by a sandy beach on the sea side and mountains on the interior. The tillable land consisted of rice paddies and farms which grew sweet potatoes and vegetables such as onions, radishes, beans, and cabbages. Farms varied in size from one or two to twenty-six acres. Several horses could be hired for plowing. Men and women shared in the agricultural work

*The cultures in which the children of our sample grew up are described in *Six Cultures: Studies of Child Rearing* (B. Whiting, ed., 1963). The individual field teams have recorded in this volume the economy, social structure, political organization, religion, and health practices, as well as the daily life of the families, their expectations and values and socialization practices. In this book we will discuss in detail only those aspects of the culture which seem to be directly related to the types of social interaction recorded in the observations of the children's behavior.

and also in lumbering on the mountains. Building material and firewood were sold to provide the family with cash income.

The weather in Taira was temperate, the daily range in winter being 55–67°F, in summer 77–89°F. The village was compact, with streets laid out in a rectangular grid (see Figure 1). The houses raised about two feet above the ground, were of wood, with plank floors and thatched or tile roofs. The simplest and most usual floor plan consisted of a living room across the front of the house, with sliding panels that made it possible to open the whole front of the house during the warm daylight hours (see Figure 2). The houses were close together, and neighbors could converse without leaving their homes. The furniture included a low table on which food was served. Members of the household, which might include grandparents, slept on the floor on mats. Every house had a kerosene lamp or two and, if there were schoolchildren, a simple desk and chair.

Okinawa has had extensive contact with both China and Japan since the seventh century. Until the late nineteenth century, there was a kingdom and royal court on the southern part of the island. Although Taira, in the mountainous area to the north, was isolated from the court, at various times during the fifteenth and sixteenth centuries noble families fled north for political reasons and chose the village as a residence. Since the Japanese takeover in the nineteenth century, Taira has been drawn into the political structure of the island, and is now connected to Naha, the capital city, by a road and bus line with daily service. Japanese has become the language of instruction in the schools. Okinawan is still spoken in the home, but since education is universal the younger generation are all bilingual.

William and Corinne Nydegger lived in Tarong in the northwest of the island of Luzon in the Philippines. The families of the children

12

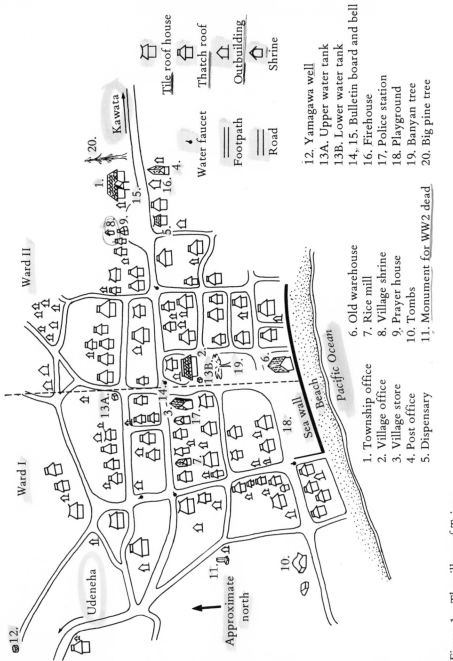

Figure 1. The village of Taira.

Tile roof house
Thatch roof
Outbuilding
Shrine
Water faucet
Footpath
Road

1. Township office
2. Village office
3. Village store
4. Post office
5. Dispensary
6. Old warehouse
7. Rice mill
8. Village shrine
9. Prayer house
10. Tombs
11. Monument for WW2 dead
12. Yamagawa well
13A. Upper water tank
13B. Lower water tank
14, 15. Bulletin board and bell
16. Firehouse
17. Police station
18. Playground
19. Banyan tree
20. Big pine tree

Ward I
Ward II
Udeneha
Kawata
Approximate north
Sea wall
Beach
Pacific Ocean

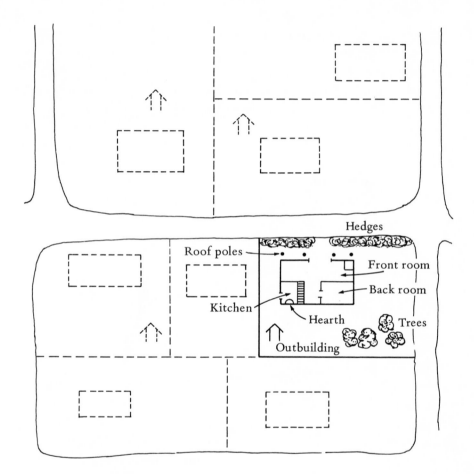

Figure 2. A typical houseplan in Taira.

small village

they studied lived in hamlets scattered over an area a mile square
which consisted of narrow curving valleys running down to the sea
and twisting ridges which are the foothills of the inland mountains.
The houses were located on the ridges, the gardens on the slopes, and
the rice paddies in the valleys. The weather was sunny and dry from
December through May, rainy in June and July, and cool in August
and September. The temperature ranged from 59° to as high as 101°
in the hottest month.

Tarongans grew both wet and dry rice as a staple and raised vegetables, tobacco, sugar cane, and fruit. Men and women worked
together in the field. Men also managed the carabao (water buffalo)
and plows and maintained the dikes of the rice paddies. Seasonal
employment on large farms outside the area and the sale of surplus
vegetables furnished cash for the families.

The houses, elevated five or six feet above the ground, had bamboo
walls and thatched roofs. The floor plan included two rectangular
units separated by a porch and storeroom (see Figure 4). The larger
rectangle included a bedroom separated by movable partitions; the
smaller housed the kitchen. Houses faced on a shared yard, with two
to six families using the common space. These families were usually
related—married brothers and their parents, married sisters and brothers, or parents of both husband and wife. Several yard groups formed
a *sitio* (see Figure 3), and sitios were combined to form *barrios*, the
smallest political unit. Rural barrios contained between fifty and a
hundred houses. Each barrio was in the charge of an elected lieuten-
ant, who was confirmed by the municipal government but for
authority had to depend on his personality.

STUDY

interesting

The Tarongans spoke Ilocano, but the language of instruction in
the schools, which most barrio children attended for at least four

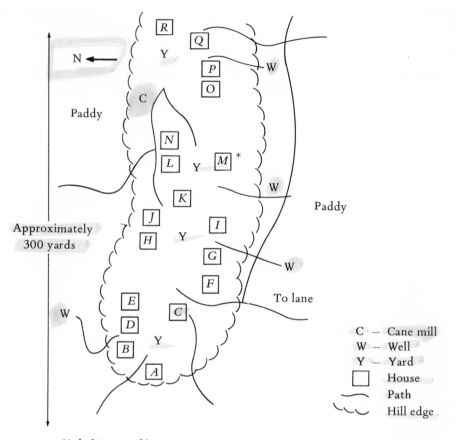

*Inhabitants of house *M* moved in with members of house *N*
to provide quarters for the anthropologists

Figure 3. The village of Tarong.

ʌ Several yard groups formed
a sitio, and sitios
were combined to form
barrios, the smallest political
unit, . . .

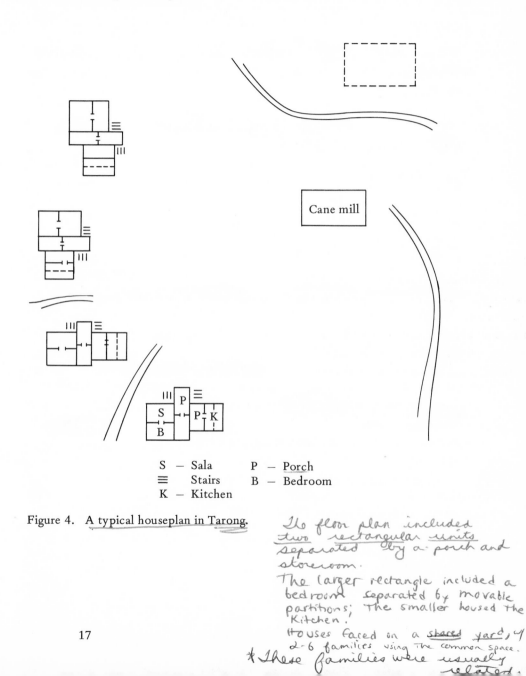

S — Sala   P — Porch
≡   Stairs   B — Bedroom
K — Kitchen

Figure 4. A typical houseplan in Tarong.

The floor plan included
two rectangular units
separated by a porch and
storeroom.
The larger rectangle included a
bedroom separated by movable
partitions; The smaller housed the
Kitchen.
Houses faced on a shared yard, 4
2-6 families using The common space.
* These families were usually
related.

years, was English. Catholicism was introduced by the Spanish, but except for baptisms, weddings, and funerals, contacts with the church were rare.

Khalapur, one of the Cornell University project villages, was in northern India, located on the fertile alluvial plain of the Ganges River in the state of Uttar Pradesh. It was one of the many thousand villages in this ancient center of civilization. Part of the Hindu kingdoms and empires until the thirteenth century, it was conquered by Islamic invaders from western Asia, and since then has been influenced by Muslim culture. Delhi, the nearest large city, was about ninety miles south.

Leigh Minturn and John Hitchcock* worked in Khalapur. The families from which the sample children came were Rajput—traditionally of the warrior caste, but farmers at the time of the study. Members of other castes lived in the town and carried on their traditional specialized occupations. The married Rajput women were in purdah, confined for most of their child-bearing years to courtyards surrounded by high mud walls. Large extended families, sometimes including four generations, lived together, with the women sharing the courtyard and windowless rooms which lined one or two sides of the open space (see Figure 6) and the men sleeping in separate quarters often two or three blocks away in the crowded, compact village (see Figure 5).

The climate was monsoonal with hot, wet summers, warm winters, and very hot, dry springs. In April and May a dust-laden wind blew in from the western desert and the temperature during the day might

---

*John Hitchcock was the director of the Cornell University field station in Khalapur. Leigh Minturn worked out of this unit and collaborated with Hitchcock in collecting the background data which is included in the monograph on the Rajputs of Khalapur.

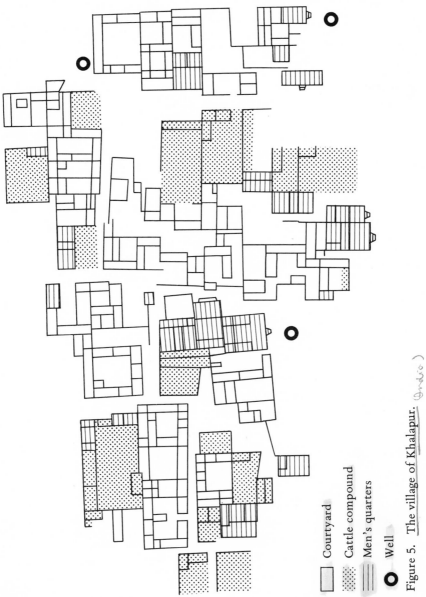

Figure 5. The village of Khalapur. (Andro)

Courtyard

Cattle compound

Men's quarters

Well

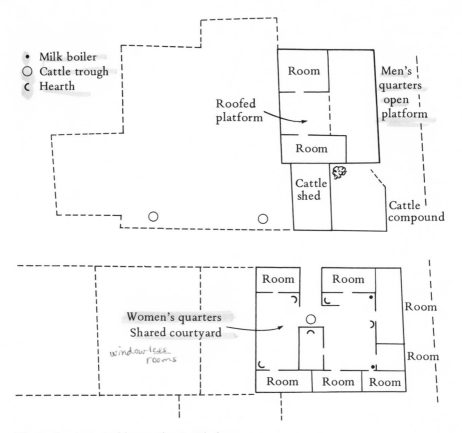

- • Milk boiler
- ○ Cattle trough
- ⊂ Hearth

Room

Men's quarters open platform

Roofed platform

Room

Cattle shed

Cattle compound

Room   Room

Room

Women's quarters
Shared courtyard

window-less rooms

Room

Room   Room   Room

Figure 6. A typical houseplan in Khalapur.

hover around 110°. The yearly range was from an absolute low of 31° in January to 115° in June.

Unlike their counterparts in Taira and Tarong, the Rajput women did not work in the fields nor did they tend the cattle which furnished dairy products for the families, although they occasionally

[handwritten:] Unlike their counterparts in Taira + Tarong, the Rajput women did NOT work in the fields, nor did they tend cattle which furnished dairy products for the families, although they occasionally helped w/ milking

20

helped with milking. Wheat and sugar cane were staples; maize, rice, millet, cotton, hemp, barley, oats, and peas and other vegetable and fodder crops were grown. Plows were drawn by bullocks, and crops transported in bullock carts from the fields which radiated out from the town. Surplus crops were traded or sold for cash.

There were both a boys' and a girls' school in Khalapur; however, although the Rajput belonged to a culture with a long tradition of art, music, and literature, a high percentage of the families were illiterate and not all children attended school. Religious observances were important in the lives of the women. All the families were Hindu, and Brahmin priests visited the courtyards for family ceremonies.

Although tied into the central government of India, at the time of the study the Rajput families still settled many of their disputes in their own local village courts called *panchayats*. The caste system had been outlawed, but distinctions of wealth, prestige, and power still differentiated the traditional occupational groups. Wealth and prestige distinctions even existed within the Rajput families of the sample.

The Nyansongo of Kenya were also agriculturalists, living in the fertile highlands of western Kenya. Their scattered homesteads were on a ridge of hills, the farms and pastures sloping down to a river which furnished the families with water (see Figure 7). Maize and beans were the staple crops and women the main farm laborers. The fields were tilled by their mattocks, there being no plows or tractors.

Nyansongo was a sublocation of the Gusii, a tribe speaking a Bantu language. They were originally predominantly herdsmen but although they valued cattle more than land, rapid population growth and the resulting scarcity of land had curtailed the size of herds. Deprived of their traditional occupation, the men found themselves with little to

21

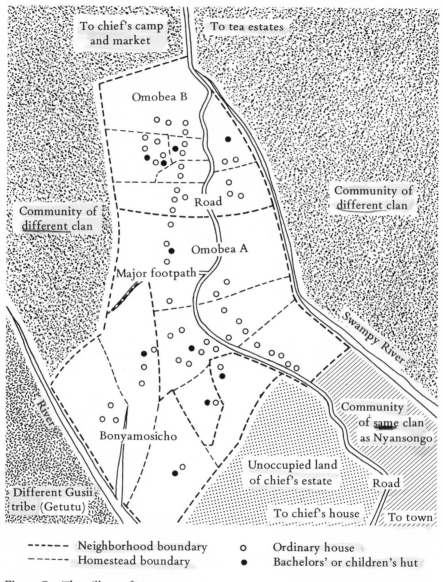

To chief's camp and market

To tea estates

Omobea B

Community of different clan

Community of different clan

Road

Omobea A

Major footpath

Swampy River

River

Community of same clan as Nyansongo

Bonyamosicho

Unoccupied land of chief's estate

Road

Different Gusii tribe (Getutu)

To chief's house

To town

------ Neighborhood boundary   o   Ordinary house
------ Homestead boundary   ●   Bachelors' or children's hut

Figure 7. The village of Nyansongo.

do outside of politicking unless they took wage-earning jobs in nearby towns or on the tea plantations or joined the army or police force. Many Nyansongo men were polygynists. Each wife had her own hut, and a man with sufficient means also had a separate one of his own. *many Nyansongo men were polygynists.*

The area had two rainy seasons—the "long" rains in April, May, and June, and the "short" rains in September and October. The temperature ranged from below 60° in the rainy seasons to above 80° in the dry seasons. Much of the daily life took place in the yard in front of the mud and wattle houses (see Figure 8). People sat under the overhanging eaves of the conical thatched roofs, and children played between the drying maize, keeping the chickens from eating the grain.

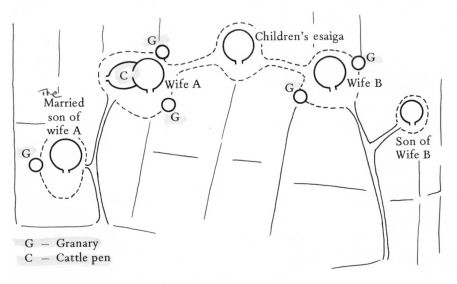

G — Granary
C — Cattle pen

Figure 8. A typical houseplan in Nyansongo. *(study)*

23

When Robert LeVine and Barbara Lloyd were living in Keumbu, near the chief's compound about four miles from the community, much of the social control resided in the elders and the chief. Although nominally under the central colonial government, the group had a high degree of autonomy: the lineage elders controlled their members, and the chief and elders supervised concerns involving several lineages.

Most of the families of the sample children were at least nominal members of one of several Christian churches, but for many the religion was but a possible source of education, for in pre-independent Kenya the missions ran the only schools. But because these schools required money for uniforms at least and because the Nyansongans were not yet strongly linked into a wage economy, few children received any education.

The community studied by A. Kimball and Romaine Romney was in the western highlands of the Mexican state of Oaxaca. It, too, was dependent on subsistence agriculture. The sample families were Mixtecan-speaking Indians who lived in the barrio of Santo Domingo in Juxtlahuaca, a ladino (Spanish-speaking) town.

The closely spaced barrio houses had partially enclosed courtyards often shared with the grandparental generation and/or married siblings or sometimes nonrelatives (see Figure 9). The farms were on the slopes beyond the town. Women did not work in the fields, although some had vegetable patches and others grew maize and beans —the staple crops—in gardens adjoining their courtyards. The houses were one-room rectangular adobe structures with tile roofs, with the kitchen in a separate structure under a thatched roof (see Figure 10). Some families had sheep and burros, the latter useful in bringing crops and firewood in from the hills.

May through September were rainy months in the western Mexican highlands. The warmest months were June, July, and August, with lows of 50° and highs of 86°, and a mean temperature of 70°. December, January, and February were the coldest, with days as cold as 32° and a mean temperature of 60°.

The barrio was Catholic and had the *cofradia* organization found throughout the area for the purpose of sponsoring celebrations in honor of various saints. Men and women cooperated in planning these fiestas, the women furnishing the specially prepared food.

Many of the adult males had been away for one or two years as migrant workers to earn cash income for their families. The women contributed to the family budget by selling tortillas or surplus maize in the market.

The children who attended school left the security of their barrio and entered the ladino part of town. At the time of the Romneys' study, the Mixtecans were treated as an inferior minority. The language of instruction in the school was Spanish.

The sixth community, studied by John and Ann Fischer, was a section in a New England town of 5,000 inhabitants. The families were predominantly members of a Baptist Church group. Unlike those in the other samples, Orchard Town fathers were not farmers but wage earners, salaried or self-employed. The children lived in single-family dwellings with many rooms, large yards, and all the conveniences of American middle-class culture (see Figures 11 and 12). The children all attended school and belonged to other child-centered groups such as the Boy and Girl Scouts. A few of the mothers had part-time jobs, but spent most of their time caring for their husbands and children and maintaining their houses and property.

During the cold winter months, when the mean temperature ranged

25

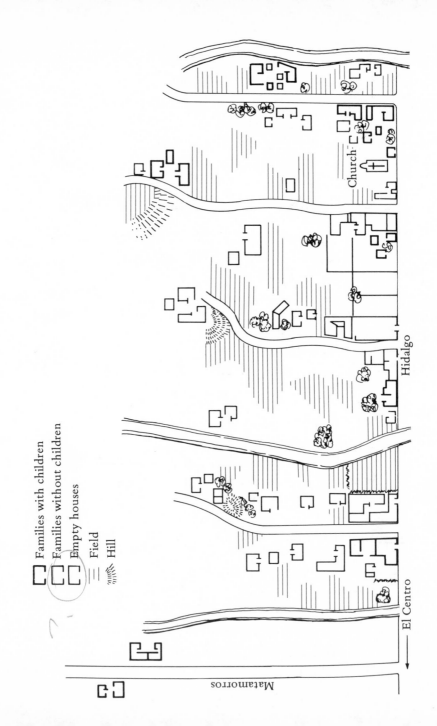

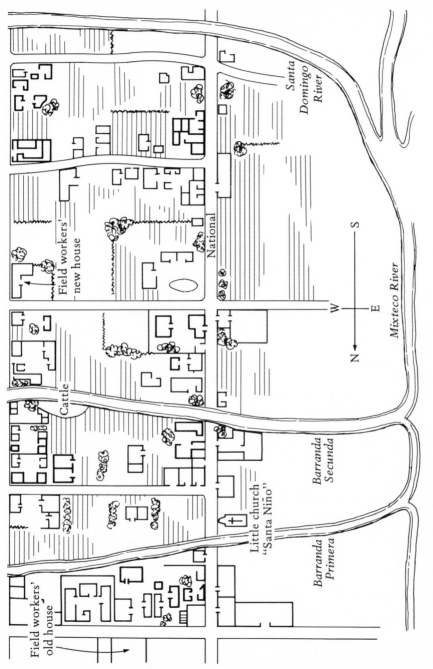

Figure 9. The village of Juxtlahuaca. (Mexico)

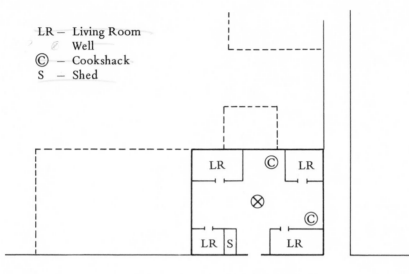

LR — Living Room
   Well
© — Cookshack
S — Shed

Figure 10. A typical houseplan in Juxtlahuaca.

from below zero to slightly above freezing, much of the life of the women and children was spent indoors. Television, games, books, and paper, pencil, and crayon projects helped keep the preschool children occupied. The men returned from work between 5 and 7 P.M. In order to see other adults during the day the women had to make special visits, bundling children up in snowsuits and boots.

During the months when they could play outdoors, preschool children were confined to their own or a neighbor's yard, since the automobile traffic on the streets, and particularly on the highway which ran through the area, was dangerous. The temperature range during

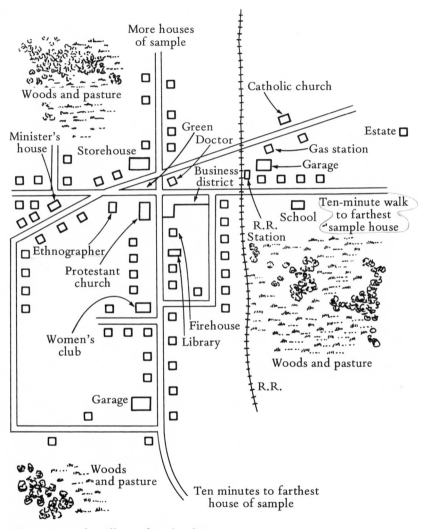

Figure 11. The village of Orchard Town.

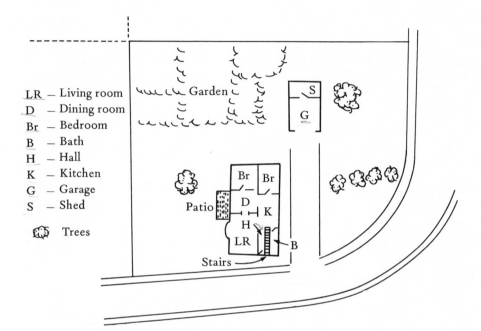

LR — Living room
D — Dining room
Br — Bedroom
B — Bath
H — Hall
K — Kitchen
G — Garage
S — Shed

🌳 Trees

Figure 12. A typical houseplan in Orchard Town.

these months was between 63° and 80°, with July usually the hottest month.

Concerned Orchard Town citizens had a chance to express their opinions and vote for town officers at town meetings. The majority of the government, however, was in the hands of delegated officials and the average citizen paid little attention except when special issues arose.

SAMPLE

The total sample consisted of sixty-seven girls and sixty-seven boys between the ages of three and eleven. There were four sex-age groups:

boys from three through six and from seven through eleven, and girls from the same age groups. In Juxtlahuaca only five older boys and girls were studied. Robert LeVine and Barbara Lloyd observed only four children in each age group in Nyansongo; they added eight children, ten through sixteen years of age, in the hope of discovering the effects of initiation. They interviewed these older children, but since they did not systematically observe their behavior, they are not included in this sample.

The selection of children was made on the basis of census material mailed to Cambridge, Massachusetts. In every case the field workers tried to locate a group of families which lived in the same neighborhood, interacted with each other, and knew the names of each others' children. It was hoped that in this way we would be able to select children whose mothers shared beliefs, values, and practices about the rearing of children.

In Taira sixty-three households were visited and census material collected. This group included 330 individuals. In Tarong it was necessary to include six adjoining sitios. In all, fifty-eight households and approximately 298 individuals were included. In Khalapur, population 5,000, the census material was gathered in thirty-eight courtyards. These courtyards were in a residential and political district known as a *patti* (clan). The census recorded approximately 361 individuals for these courtyards. In Nyansongo eighteen contiguous homesteads were censused, including 208 individuals. The families all belonged to one clan and neighboring homesteads often belonged to the same lineage. In Juxtlahuaca, population 3,600, a census was made of thirty-one courtyards in the Mixtecan barrio of the town. The total population of the barrio was around 600, and the courtyards included about half this figure. In Orchard Town, population 5,000, a census was made of forty-two households, most of whom lived on three adjoining streets in North Village (population 1,600). The census included 195 people.

In sum, in four of the societies the twenty-four children were chosen from about three hundred individuals. In the other two the universe included around two hundred people.

The selection of the sample was made in Cambridge to avoid the possibility that the field teams would draw a biased sample by choosing salient or appealing children. To maximize the independence of cases not more than one child was selected from each household. The children were chosen on the basis of sex and age group. Attempts to match by actual age, sibling order, number of siblings, or household type, and so on, were not feasible with the number of children available.

The distribution of the sample by sex and age is shown in Table 1. As can be seen, the subgroups are reasonably well-balanced. The ages of younger boys and girls in Tarong and older boys in Tarong and Juxtlahuaca show a discrepancy of more than a year.

The number of children in families of the samples showed considerable variation (see Table 2). Nyansongan, Juxtlahuacan, and Tairan children were brought up in the largest families; Orchard

Table 1. Mean ages for the sex-age groups in each culture.

Group	Nyan-songo	Juxtla-huaca	Tarong	Taira	Khala-pur	Orchard Town	Total
Young boys	4.8	5.0	3.8	4.8	4.8	4.7	4.7
Young girls	4.8	4.8	3.8	4.8	5.0	4.2	4.6
Older boys	9.0	7.4	7.2	9.0	9.5	8.7	8.5
Older girls	8.0	8.4	8.2	8.3	8.3	8.7	8.3

nyansongan, juxtalahuacan,
+Tairan children were brought
up in the largest families.

Table 2. Distribution of the number of living children per family in the sample.

Number of children	Nyan-songo	Juxtla-huaca	Tarong	Taira	Khala-pur	Orchard Town	Total
1	1	0	2	0	2	2	7
2	3	1	7	3	7	8	29
3	3	6	5	5	3	6	28
4	3	9	2	9	5	5	33
5	4	4	4	6	4	2	23
6	1	0	1	1	1	1	6
7	0	1	1	0	2	0	4
8	1	1	0	0	0	0	2
9	0	0	2	0	0	0	2
Median	4	4	3	4	3-4	3	4

Town and Tarongan in the smallest. For the whole sample the typical (modal) family consisted of four children. The range was greatest in Nyansongo where one family had but one child and another had nine. Tarong, Juxtlahuaca, and Khalapur each had one or two families with seven or more children. The largest family in both Taira and Orchard Town had six.

The median age of the mothers varied from thirty to thirty-seven years, the oldest in Orchard Town. Juxtlahuacan and Tarongan mothers were on the young side, Tairan and Tarongan mothers older. Khalapur not only had the youngest mother, an eighteen-year-old, but also the oldest, fifty-five years of age.

The six cultures also varied in the number of children in various positions in the sibling order. This is shown in Table 3. Orchard Town and Khalapur deviate from the others in the high proportion of youngest and only children. For the rest of the sample more of the children

Table 3. Number of children in each position by sibling order.

Sibling order	Nyan-songo	Juxtla-huaca	Tarong	Taira	Khala-pur	Orchard Town	Total
Youngest	3	3	4	2	8	12	32
Middle	8	10	10	15	7	5	54
Oldest	4	9	8	7	6	5	41
Only	1	0	2	0	3	2	6

were in the middle of the sibling order than in any other position. Juxtlahuaca has the highest proportion of oldest children.

As Table 4 indicates, the majority—slightly over 60 percent—of the children in the sample were brought up in nuclear households consisting of mothers, fathers, and sometimes an unmarried uncle or aunt. This was the predominant pattern in three of the cultures: Juxtlahuaca, Tarong, and Orchard Town. The lineal household in which a son or daughter continues to live with their parents after marriage was next most common; this type of household predominated in Taira. Fifteen children lived in extended households, distinguished from lineal by the inclusion of a married uncle or aunt as well as one or more grandparents. The large atrium houses in Khalapur were most likely to accommodate this group of kinsmen. The most unusual arrangement, found only in Nyansongo, was the polygynous household occupied by a mother, unmarried daughters, her younger sons, and sometimes her husband.

The rules of residence were prescriptively based on patrilineal descent in both Nyansongo and Khalapur; the parents and married brothers of the father formed the basis of extended and lineal family groupings in these cultures. In Taira ideally the eldest son stayed on with his parents after his marriage; but perhaps due to dislocation

[handwritten annotation: as table 4 indicates, the majority — slightly over 60% — of the children in the sample were brought up in nuclear households consisting of mothers, fathers, and sometimes an unmarried uncle or aunt.]

Table 4. Distribution of household types for the sample children.

	Nyan-songo	Juxtla-huaca	Tarong	Taira	Khala pur	Orchard Town	Total
Nuclear[a]	6	19	19	11	8[d]	23	86
Lineal[b]	0	3	4	12	3	1	23
Extended[c]	0	0	1	1	13	0	15
Polygynous	10	0	0	0	0	0	10

[a] Nuclear households consist of a mother, her children, and her husband if monogamously married. (Unmarried brothers and sisters of the mother or father sometimes live in these households. In a few instances the father was either deceased or working away.)

[b] A *lineal* household consists of a grandmother and/or grandfather together with one married son or daughter. *[handwritten annotation: — son or daughter continues to live w/ their parents after marriage.]*

[c] An *extended* household consists of a grandmother and/or grandfather together with two or more married sons and/or daughters or two or more married brothers or sisters and their children. *[handwritten annotation: distinguished from lineal by the inclusion of a married uncle or aunt as well as one or more grandparent]*

[d] Household types are difficult to classify in Khalapur because of the half walls which were built down the middle of courtyards when there were family quarrels. A family has been arbitrarily classified as nuclear if the wall was built before 1955. A household is defined here as family members who sleep under the same roof or, in the case of Khalapur, kin who share the same women's courtyard. This is not the same classification as published earlier (B. Whiting, 1963; Minturn and Lambert, 1964).

during the war, four of the thirteen lineal families included the wife's mother rather than the husband's. In the other cultures there were no such prescriptive rules and either a partilineal or matrilineal or bilocal basis might be used. In our sample a patrilineal basis was preferred in Juxtlahuaca, fourteen to five. There was no clear pattern in the Tarong or Orchard Town samples, although the former professed to prefer patrilocal residence.

Forty-three percent of the children of the sample were living in the house or yard with someone of the grandparental generation (see

Table 5). Sometimes a greataunt or greatuncle represented that generation. In twenty-seven instances the grandparental generation included males and females; in twenty-three instances females only; and in seven males only. The general tendency of the women to marry earlier and live longer than the men presumably accounts for this preponderance of females. The distribution of grandparents by culture reflects not only the pattern of extended and lineal families but also the difference between prescriptive and permissive residency rules. The probability of there being a living, residential grandparent was twice as great in Taira, Juxtlahuaca, and Tarong, where the parents of either the father or mother may live in the household or yard group, than in Nyansongo and Khalapur, where only the father's parents were eligible, or Orchard Town, where neither was welcome. The percentage of the sample children living in three-generation compounds in each culture reflects these differences. Because most Khalapur families were lineal or extended, it might be expected that more than a third of the children would come from three-generational families; the fact that of the thirteen extended families eight had no one of the grandparental generation in residence accounts for this apparent discrepancy.

Exogamous rules governing marriage also effect the availability of grandmothers. In Taira, Tarong, Juxtlahuaca, and Orchard Town an additional twenty-three grandmothers were within easy walking or driving distance of their grandchildren (six, five, five, and seven, respectively), while in Khalapur and Nyansongo, where a man must marry outside of his village or localized lineage, there were none.

There is considerable variation with regard to the number of kin-related children readily available as playmates (see Table 6). Most children in Tarong, Juxtlahuaca, and Nyansongo had six or more

Table 5. Presence of grandparents living in the house or yard of the sample children.[a]

	Nyan-songo	Juxtla-huaca	Tarong	Taira	Khala-pur	Orchard Town	Total
Grandfather	0	1	1	1	3	1	7
Grandmother	1	5	6	8	2	1	23
Both	3	5	11	4	3	1	27
Neither	12	11	6	11	16	21	79
Percentage of one or both present	25	50	75	54	33	8	43

[a]Step-grandparents, greataunts, and greatuncles have been included.

Table 6. Distribution of kin-related children in the household and/or yards of the sample.

Number of kin-related children[a]	Nyan-songo	Juxtla-huaca	Tarong	Taira	Khala-pur	Orchard Town
0	1	0	0	0	0	2
1	1	0	4	2	1	7
2	1	0	0	6	1	7
3	0	4	2	10	3	4
4	1	4	2	3	4	2
5	1	1	1	1	6	1
6	4	5	4	0	3	0
7	3	2	3	0	2	0
8	1	3	2	0	1	0
9	0	3	0	0	0	0
10	0	0	2	0	2	0
10 and over	2	0	4	0	1	0
Median	6	6	6	3	5	2

[a]Children are defined as being unmarried and under 19 if male or under 17 if female. Kinsmen include siblings, half-siblings, cousins, uncles, and aunts.

The general tendency of the women to marry earlier + live longer than the men presumably accounts for this preponderance of females.

37

siblings, half-siblings, cousins, uncles, or aunts living in the same house or yard. By contrast, one-third of the children in Orchard Town had either one or no such playmates. Five is both the median and the mode for the whole sample.

In sum, the samples are balanced by sex and age only; with respect to family size, sibling order, and residence patterns there is considerable variation from culture to culture.

3   Method

BEHAVIOR OBSERVATIONS

A plan for collecting observations of children's behavior in a systematic manner was worked out by field teams, the senior investigators, and a number of consultants during a six-week session held in the summer before the field work began.* Because its details are reported in the *Field Guide* (Whiting et al., 1966), there is no need to do more than summarize them here. The procedure for data analysis and coding, however, will be explained fully.

Several rules governed the procedure for collecting the descriptions of the social interactions of the sample children. First, because our theoretical interest was social interaction we decided to ignore solitary or autistic behavior and to focus attention on the behavior of P (the sample child) and others with whom he or she was interacting and to record sequences which included both the instigations to P's acts and their effect on others. Second, our pretests indicated that

*The names of the consultants are given in the Preface.

reliability decreases rapidly with fatigue, so we decided upon a five-minute behavior sample. Third, the work of Barker and Wright (1954) indicated the importance of setting in influencing behavior; therefore, a plan of setting sampling was formulated. Finally, previous research on children's social behavior (Sears, Maccoby, and Levin, 1957; Whiting and Child, 1953) suggested that there were a number of transcultural categories that could be presumed to describe social interaction, and we decided to focus our attention on these. They were nurturance, succorance, sociability, achievement, dominance, submission, aggression, responsibility, and self-reliance. On the basis of available evidence, however, we felt it would be dangerous to assume that these categories would be applicable in all six societies without modification; we therefore determined to take descriptive protocols and to use the nine categories to set boundaries for and to exemplify the domain in which we were interested. Most of these predetermined procedures were followed by each field team.

As planned, the observers first mapped the daily routine of boys and girls in the two age groups. They followed the children around, noting their presence in different settings at different times of the day. They recorded the activities in progress in these settings and supplemented their observations by interviews with the adults and the children.

Having established the daily routine, the observers began collecting specimens of behavior of the sample children. First, they located a sample child, and noted the time of day, place, and group of people present. Each person was classified by age, sex, and kinship to the sample child and household membership. The activity of the group was ascertained. This initial process took at least five minutes. The observer then wrote down the time and began to watch the sample child (P) and record his or her behavior. An attempt was made to note all stimuli affecting P so as to be able to attempt an assessment of the instigations of P's behavior. In order to do this the observer tried to follow the child's eyes and look where P focused his or her attention. If, for example, a group of children were interacting, the description would not include detailed accounts of the behavior of anyone who was apparently not being noticed by the sample child. The observations were recorded in English nouns, verbs, and pronouns with a minimal number of interpretive qualifiers.*

The observer noted when five minutes had elapsed, but if the episode in progress was particularly interesting, he or she continued the observation until it was finished. The observer was accompanied by a bilingual assistant who transcribed all verbal communications. No more than one observation was made on a child per day to prevent oversampling of behavior influenced by minor illness or emotional disturbances, and each child was observed a minimum of fourteen times (a total of seventy minutes) over a period lasting several months to a year. Table 7 shows the average number of observations per child. Only the first five minutes were analyzed in observations which continued beyond the standard period, and only this time is included in the mean number of minutes per child.

To observe the sample child's behavior and focus of attention required unusually close attention and did not allow for writing a full protocol. Thus, a full protocol could not be written concurrently. Notes were taken at this time, and the protocol was rewritten in detail as soon as possible. If the observation was made by two people in collaboration, they discussed and collated both sets of notes.

*The exception was Juxtlahuaca, where protocols were first recorded in Spanish and then translated into English.

Table 7. Average number of observations per child and minutes of observation per child.

	Nyan- songo	Juxtla- huaca	Tarong	Taira	Khala- pur	Orchard Town
Observations per child	15	15.7	27	14.7	19	16.4
Minutes per child	75	79	135	74	95	82

Originally we had intended to compute the reliability of our measures by having two observers record the same child's behavior and compare protocols. This turned out to be impractical. With the exception of New England, the observer had to be accompanied by a bilingual assistant, an essential aid to the fieldworker in interpreting the subtleties of the language, the meaning of gestures, and so on. Since only one assistant was available at any one time at a field site, it was impossible to make simultaneous observations; hence the question of reliability must be taken on faith.

SAMPLING THE SETTING

Although the research plan called for the sampling of settings in proportion to the time they were occupied (Whiting et al., 1966, pp. 91–94), this proved impractical. It was too time-consuming to find the children in certain settings, and they were too self-conscious when the observers' presence was more obtrusive because of the nature of the setting. The Maretzkis, for example, found it awkward to observe in the Tairan houses; the Fischers found it difficult to find children except at home or at school or at Scouts or Sunday school. Few observations were made in the evenings in any of the societies.

Table 8 gives the percentages of observations made in the various settings. It can be seen that with the exception of Taira the majority were made in the house or yard or in the area immediately adjacent. These percentages are the means for all the children. Computed for just the three-through six-year-old age groups, 80 to 90 percent of the observations were made in the house and/or courtyard in Orchard Town, Tarong, and Juxtlahuaca. In every case but that of the young girls in Taira and the older boys in Orchard Town and Tarong, girls were observed at home slightly more frequently than boys. The sex difference increased with age, being greatest in the courtyard societies of Khalapur (37 percent of the observations of older boys made in the courtyard as compared with 75 percent of those of the older girls) and Juxtlahuaca (40 percent of the older boys and 65 percent of the older girls). Since observers, when looking for P, went first to the

Table 8. Percentage of observations according to location.

Location	Nyan-songo (Kenya)	Juxtla-huaca (Mexico)	Tarong (Philippines)	Taira (Japan)	Khala-pur (N. India)	Orchard Town (New England)
House or yard	57	72	74	32	72	76
Adjacent pasture or garden	31	0	0	0	0	0
School and school playground	0	8	21	12	10	14
Other public places	12	20	5	56	18	10

[handwritten marginalia: Since observer, when looking for P, went first to the child's home. This difference reflects the fact that in all of the societies, girls remained closer to home. It can be seen that w/ the exception of Taira the majority were made in the house or yard or in the area immediately adjacent.]

43

Boys at play, Khalapur

child's home, this difference reflects the fact that in all of the societies girls remain closer to home, a finding replicated in a recent study by Sara Nerlove in Nyansongo (1969) and by the Munroes among the Luhya in Kenya (Nerlove, Munroe, and Munroe, 1971).

An adult was present most frequently in Orchard Town; next most frequently in Khalapur, Tarong, and Juxtlahuaca; and least frequently in Nyansongo and Taira. Table 9 shows the percentage of observations in which the mother was present. The proportions for four of the cultures are virtually identical, ranging between 37 and 39 percent, somewhat less for Nyansongo. Mothers were seldom present in Taira. The lower frequency in Nyansongo and Taira is to be expected, and reflects the fact that the mothers in these societies spend more time working away from the dwelling. However, the extremely low frequency in Taira is also the result of the Maretzkis' reluctance to observe inside the houses. Fathers are present considerably less often than mothers. Grandmothers were observed most frequently in Tarong, where there were more grandmothers who lived within easy walking distance.

Table 10 summarizes the percentage of time a sample child was with various categories of children. Its figures reflect not only the

Table 9. Percentage of observations in which an adult was present.

Present	Nyan-songo	Juxtla-huaca	Tarong	Taira	Khala-pur	Orchard Town
Any adult	57	68	72	39	73	84
Mother	32	38	41	9	37	47
Father	10	9	14	3	3	9
Grandmother	5	7	14	4	7	1

Table 10. Percentage of observations in which housemates, courtyard cousins, outsiders, and children of the same sex exclusively were present in the observations of sample children.

Type present	Nyan-songo (Kenya)	Juxtla-huaca (Mexico)	Tarong (Philippines)	Taira (Japan)	Khala-pur (India)	Orchard Town (New England)
Housemates	63	63	56	46	43	33
Courtyard cousins	40	29	39	1	4[a]	1
Outsiders	3	20	22	82	29	25
Same sex groups	32	28	25	31	33	33

[a] Since Khalapur households are extended, housemates include cousins; in other societies housemates are almost exclusively siblings.

kinship composition of play groups, but their stability. Children who appeared in protocols were classified on the basis of kinship relations and place of residence. Those who did not live within easy walking distance were classified as outsiders. Nyansongon and Juxtlahuacan children were with siblings most frequently. In both of these societies children are encouraged to stay inside the homestead and courtyard. Nyansongan children were rarely with outsiders. In Khalapur and Orchard Town children spent less than half their time with siblings and courtyard cousins, and one-fourth their time with outsiders. Over three-fourths of the Tairan observations were with outsiders. In sum, play groups were most stable in Nyansongo, Juxtlahuaca, and Tarong; in the first two because parents put pressure on the children to keep it so, and in Tarong because the clusters of houses were dispersed and the yard groups afforded the most

46

Children playing house, Taira

[NOTE]

accessible playmates. All the children in Taira and Khalapur and the
older children in Orchard Town were freer to wander away from
home to find friends and to change play groups. Taira is the most
open, its play groups the most fluid.

Although children are not completely free to choose their friends
and playmates, being confined by both ecology and rules to restricted
areas and sometimes required to care for younger siblings, it is
interesting that in nearly one-third of the observations (see Table 10)
children were observed associating with children of the same sex,
the range being from 25 percent in Tarong to 33 percent in Khalapur
and Orchard Town. That this reflects a universal affinity is further
indicated by the fact that roughly 65 percent of the targets of the
coded social acts of sample children were of the same sex.

Table 11 shows the character of the child's dominant activity during observations. Play may be organized or unstructured, individual
or as part of a group. Work may be individual or carried on as a member of a group. All protocols which had neither work, play, or
learning as a central activity were classified as casual social inter-

Table 11 Percentage of observations made during various activities.

Activity	Nyan-songo (Kenya)	Juxtla-huaca (Mexico)	Tarong (Philippines)	Taira (Japan)	Khala-pur (India)	Orchard Town (New England)
Play	17	49	48	76	31	52
Casual social interaction	43	37	31	11	46	30
Work	41	8	14	9	11	2
Learning	0	6	7	4	9	16

[handwritten margin notes: STUDY; protocol preliminary record; p.55 → Samples of beh. in ¶ form; all protocols which had neither work, play, or learning as a central activity were classified as casual social interaction.]

After school in Orchard Town

action. Tairan children were observed playing more than other children and Nyansongan children less. Casual social interaction was highest in Khalapur and Nyansongo and lowest in Taira. Nyansongan children were observed working four times as frequently as most children, the children of Tarong ranking next but only a third as frequently. Learning settings were most frequent in Orchard Town observations—which simply reflects the fact that the Fischers made more observations in classrooms than the other field workers.

There is a striking similarity among the six cultures in the size of the small groups (eight and under) in which the sample children were observed, but the cultures varied considerably in the frequency with which children were observed in larger groups. As shown in Table 12, groups of four were typical for Nyansongo, Juxtlahuaca, Tarong, and Khalapur. A group composed of five was more common for

Table 12. Percentage of observations made when P was participating in groups of varying size.

Number of persons in setting	Nyan-songo (Kenya)	Juxtla-huaca (Mexico)	Tarong (Philippines)	Taira (Japan)	Khala-pur (India)	Orchard Town (New England)
2	7	6	8	1	7	8
3	17	14	12	10	15	24
4	22[a]	21	16	12	18	20
5	19	18	14	19	15	8
6	14	13	14	15	10	5
7	9	12	10	12	8	3
8	2	3	5	5	3	1
9 and over	3	13	20	19	12	25

[a]Italicized figures indicate the modal value for each column.

Boys at play, Tarong

Children at play, Orchard Town

Children playing, Juxtlahuaca (mexico)

Taira, of three for Orchard Town. In every case, however, the frequencies were normally distributed for various group sizes up to eight. The number of observations made in larger groups varied from 25 percent for Orchard Town to 3 percent for Nyansongo.

CODING

The samples of behavior in paragraph form (that is behavior protocols) were mailed to Cambridge, Massachusetts, where a staff of coders processed them (see Appendix C). In the initial stage each protocol was analyzed sequentially (mapped). The children with whom the sample child interacted were identified and their responses to the sample child and the sample child's response to them were coded. The code for mapping was inductively developed and consisted of seventy verbal categories and four sets of adverbial qualifiers. The adverbial qualifiers which were found to be most useful and reliable were representative of the nine behavior systems that were the focus of our study. One of the systems—achievement—did not appear in the code as a verb but only as an adverbial qualifier, for example, achievemently. Two other behavioral systems—self-reliance and responsibility—were most frequently noted by adverbs. These adverbial qualifiers also made it possible to code behavior which did not appear in the list of seventy verbs. If, for example, P performed some chore such as tending the fire, stirring the food, or sweeping the floor, his or her behavior could be noted as 00 (uncodable) in the act column with *responsibly* as an adverbial qualifier. Similarly, P might perform a nonsocial act *self-reliantly* or *aggressively* in response to some environmental or social instigation.

Two other adverbial qualifiers—compliantly and noncompliantly—made it possible to code nonsocial but theoretically relevant behavior. If, for example, a child was asked by his or her mother to perform a chore, the act in response to the mother's request, although not in the act list, could be coded as 00 with a compliant or noncompliant adverbial qualifier.

Because our primary interest was social interaction, we were concerned with coding the instigation to P's response. About half the time such instigations could be identified from the protocols; for the remainder of P's responses it was assumed that P had initiated the responses. Since instigations by others were usually social acts, the same code as that used for describing P's responses were used. Several situational instigations were added in the interest of theory; unfortunately, they occurred with such low frequency that their importance could not be determined. These situational categories were: O (another person) encounters difficulty in P's presence; O hurts self in P's presence; P encounters difficulty; P hurts self; O breaks a rule in P's presence; P encounters a situation calling for responsibility.

Since P's response by definition involved social interaction, it was always directed at some other child or adult. The coders identified these targets by sex, age, and kin relationship to P and classified their responses (the *effect* act) by the same code developed to describe P's behavior.

The mapping was done in Cambridge by personnel who were hired and trained to do the job. On an average every tenth protocol was scored by two people (partners for checking reliability were rotated). There was 87 percent agreement between coders on P's act, 75 percent on the instigating act, and 80 percent on the effect act. On the nine adverbial qualifiers which related to the behavioral systems the coders agreed 70 percent of the time. The reliability on the other three sets of adverbs was so low that they were dropped from the analysis.

When the mapping was completed, the information was transferred to a numerical code suitable for computer analysis (see Appendix B). Each act of P, together with setting variables, instigation if any, and target and effect of act, was punched on a separate IBM card. An initial tabulation indicated that approximately 20,000 acts had been identified and described for the 134 children of our sample, an average of approximately 150 acts per child.

Since we had identified seventy types of acts which could be combined with the nine behavior system adverbs, yielding a possibility of 630 subtypes, data reduction was clearly in order. Tabulation of the subtypes indicated that 90 percent of the coded acts fell into thirty-two cells. The remaining tenth consisted of categories with only one or two instances, so it was decided to omit them from further analysis. Even though the observers were instructed to focus on social interaction, five of these thirty-two categories described solitary play or work. These, representing approximately half of the recorded acts, also were dropped.

Even some of the remaining twenty-seven were of low frequency, so we decided to combine some categories. Two categories were combined if: (1) they intuitively belonged in the same theoretical category such as aggression or nurturance; (2) they were frequently used as alternatives by two different coders to describe the same behavior; and (3) they were correlated, for example, if the same child used them as alternative responses. By this process we arrived at twelve categories of behavior, plus *complies* and *does not comply* (see Appendix A).

Table 13 indicates the manner in which the twenty-seven categories were reduced to twelve. Three of the categories—*offers help, touches* (contacts physically), and *assaults sociably*—remained unchanged. The remainder were combined in some way, either on the basis of the verb, the adverbial qualifier, or a combination of the two.

Table 13. The twelve acts defined by combinations of verbs and adverbs.

Acts	Verbs	Adverbs
Seeks help	Seeks help	Any
	Suggests	Submissively
	Suggests	Succorantly
Seeks attention	Arrogates self	Any
	Seeks approval	Any
Seeks dominance	Suggests	Dominantly
	Suggests	None
Suggests responsibly	Suggests	Responsibly
	Suggests	Nurturantly
	Assaults	Responsibly
		Nurturantly
		Adult role
Offers support	Offers emotional support or affection	Any
	Gives approval	Any
Offers help	Offers help	Any
Acts sociably	Suggests	Sociably
	Greets	Any
	Acts sociably	Any
	Joins group interactions	Any
Touches	Contacts physically	Any
Reprimands	Reprimands	Any
	Warns	Any
	Threatens punishment by speaker	Responsibly/nurturantly
	Accuses of deviation	Adult role
Assaults sociably (horseplay)	Assaults	Sociably

(continued)

Table 13.   (continued)

Acts	Verbs	Adverbs
Assaults	Assaults	*Not* sociably *Not* responsibly *Not* nurturantly *Not* adult role
Symbolic aggression (insults)	Frightens	Any
	Insults	Any
	Threatens by gesture	Any
	Threatens punishment	*Not* nurturantly/*not* responsibly/*not* adult role
	Challenges to competition	Any
	Suggests	Aggressively

The final categories include six of the nine behaviors as originally described in the Field Guide (Whiting et al., 1966) and adopted from Murray (1943). Nurturance was defined in the original plan (p. 10) as follows: "In the presence of knowledge that someone else is in a state of need or drive, nurturance consists of tendencies to try to alleviate this state in another person." The empirical categories most closely corresponding to nurturance are *offers help* and *offers support*. Attempts to alleviate emotional needs or drives were classified in the latter category, other needs or drives in the former. *Offers help* includes tendering food, toys or tools, or helpful information to another. The criterion that the nurturing agent has "knowledge that someone else is in a state of need or drive" was not strictly adhered to. If the goods offered were judged to be generally useful, the act was classified as nurturance. Thus, an offer of food was considered to be nurturant even though the other said, "No thanks. I am not

Succorance = (handwritten at top)

hungry." Delousing and hair-combing, even though painful to the recipient, were also included in the *offers help* category. The state of need of the other was often more evident in the case of *offers support* than was true of *offers help*. *Offers support* frequently occurred in the protocols in response to another's crying, fright, or discouragement, though amusing a baby when it seemed perfectly happy was also included in this category. Acts of affection and approval were considered equivalent to *offers support*. *(handwritten in right margin: The state of need of the other was often more evident in the case of offers support than was true of offers help)*

Succorance was defined (p. 9) as follows: "In the presence of a drive which could be reduced either by the nurturant response of another person, or in some other way (e.g., by self-reliant behavior, cooperative interaction as equals, dominance, aggression), succorance consists of tendencies to await the nurturant response of another, accept the nurturant response of another, or signal to another the wish for nurturance." The empirical categories most closely corresponding to succorance are *seeks help* and *seeks attention*. *Seeks help*, like *offers help*, operationally included seeking material goods as well as seeking help in performing some instrumental task. *Seeks attention* included asking for approval, boasting, and showing off. "Awaiting the nurturant response of another," one of the acts theoretically specified as succorance, was seldom recorded. Most *seeks help* and *seeks attention* involved explicit verbal or gestural responses. *(handwritten in right margin: "def." ; "seeks help" ; "seeks attention")*

Sociability was defined in the *Field Guide* (p. 10) as follows: "In the presence or prospective presence of other people, especially of other people who are making a friendly approach (as if in expectation of direct reciprocation), sociability consists of tendencies to make a friendly response, to engage in activities together, and to cooperate for the sake of social interaction. (Sociability is defined to include behavior toward persons of a superior or inferior status, more or less *(handwritten in right margin: def)* needy or resourceful, providing that the behavior itself involves reciprocity as equals; however, sociability is less likely to be confused with nurturance and succorance if measured only from behavior toward peers.)" As the category of *acts sociably* developed from the data, it included greeting, exchanging information judged to express group solidarity rather than to satisfy some immediate practical need, suggesting a group game, or simply playing with other children if the action could not be scored more appropriately in some other category. In general, the category comprised friendly, but noninstrumental, social interaction. If a child asks another "Where are you going?" or "What are you doing?" these questions could be coded as *acts sociably* rather than *seeks help*. "How do you do this?" would, however, fall in the latter category.

Dominance was defined (p. 10) as follows: "In a relation with another person or group, dominance consists of tendencies to demand that the other person act in certain ways, to attempt direction of the other person's responses without making formal demands, to enforce demands, or to attain a social position which will increase facilities for enforcing demands." Dominance yielded two distinctive categories: *seeks dominance* and *suggests responsibly*. The former was used when the beneficiary of the social exchange of goods and services was the actor himself; the latter when the beneficiary was either the target or some group of which both the actor and the target were members— for example, the family if the interaction was between siblings or cousins, or the community if between nonrelatives. Thus the distinction was made between "egoistic" and "pro-social" dominance. Both types of dominance could be coded as *suggests* as the verbal designation, the distinction being made on the basis of the adverbial modifier. If the adverb was "dominantly" the observed act was coded as *seeks*

60

dominance; if it was "responsibly" or "nurturantly" the act was coded as *suggests responsibly*. A girl telling her younger brother to wash his hands because it is suppertime would be coded as *suggests responsibly*. If she tried to force him to play the part of a baby in a game she was playing it was coded as *seeks dominance*.

A distinction was made in the *Field Guide* (pp. 16–19) between "opportunity aggression" and "instrumental aggression." The former describes aggression judged to be carried out purely for the sake of hurting someone; the latter to achieve some end. Although this distinction was of great theoretical interest, it did not turn out to be very useful in the field, the reason being that pure opportunity aggression rarely occurred. The great bulk of aggression, as described by our observers, was classified as instrumental. Apparently there were few if any sadists in the sample.

Other distinctions, however, were made in the general category of aggression. Physical and symbolic acts of aggression were separated, and the former category was dichotomized on the basis of whether it was judged to be serious or playful. Three categories of aggression emerged: *assaults* (seriously); *assaults sociably* or horseplay; and *insults*.

Assaults, for example, striking or slapping someone with stick or hand, or kicking them, occurred rarely. Of the twelve categories it was the smallest, accounting for less than 3 percent of all the acts involved (see Table 14). *Assaults sociably*, although also a low frequency category, was observed to occur twice as often as *assaults*. The bulk of this category consisted of "horseplay," for example, friendly wrestling and back-slapping. *Insults* or symbolic aggression consisted of threats and insults either by word or gesture. Attempts to derogate or frighten another fell into this category. As with physical aggression,

61

Since interpretations of gestural and verbal insults are difficult w/o intimate knowledge of the culture, The coders were often unable to make the playful vs. hostile judgment. for this reason, The category combined the two types of symbolic aggression.

some insults were intended as friendly teasing, others as more serious and hostile expressions. Since interpretations of gestural and verbal insults are difficult without intimate knowledge of the culture, the coders were often unable to make the playful versus hostile judgment. For this reason the category combined the two types of symbolic aggression.

Two categories emerged that were not anticipated in the *Field Guide.* These were *reprimands* and *touches*. The former might have been included either with aggression or dominance and, as will be shown in the next chapter, partakes of both. Reprimanding behavior consisted of scolding or berating someone for what he or she had done. Children who did this often acted as though they were a parent and referred to the breaking of rules.

"reprimands" & "touches"

Touches was an ambiguous category. When children made friendly physical contact with one another, it was often difficult to judge whether they were being nurturant, succorant, or sociable. The acts consisted of embracing or patting, leaning against someone, or climbing in a lap. Like assaulting, this was an infrequently occurring category.

Note

The category *responsibility* was defined (p. 10) as follows: "In any situation in which performance of a task is required, expected, or preferred as a part of one's social role, responsibility consists of tendencies to perform the task." Since such behavior is not necessarily social in character, no act type appeared which fit this description. The performance of specific economic tasks and baby-tending, however, were coded separately and will be used in the analysis. They are an index of the responsibility expected of a child. *Suggests responsibly* often appeared as a type of social interaction when a child was engaged in such tasks, as did *reprimands*, which also implies a concern for the proper performance of one's role.

"responsibility" (def.)

? ?

62

Achievement behavior was difficult to identify in the observations. Although the children may well have been motivated by a need to achieve a standard of excellence, this could not be observed. In a few instances children were observed practicing some skill, but since this seldom if ever involved social interaction it was excluded from our analysis. Since *seeks attention* often included calling attention to some performance which the actor deemed noteworthy, this category probably comes closest to reflecting achievement motivation.

Self-reliance was defined (p. 10) as "tendencies toward self-initiation of a response sequences and toward maximum reliance upon one's own responses in reaching the goal." Although it is not one of our twelve categories of social behavior, a judgment was made as to whether each act was in response to some act of another person or self-initiated. Thus, an estimate of one aspect of *self-reliance* could be made for each child. The other aspect, "maximum reliance upon one's own responses in reaching the goal," could not be judged from the protocols. A low score on *seeks help* might be taken as an index of this aspect of *self-reliance*.

The final category specified in the *Field Guide*—obedience—was treated in a special way. Whenever a specific act was suggested or demanded of one of the children, his or her response was coded as *complies* or *does not comply*. However, since the response might also fall into one of the twelve categories, this raised the problem of double scoring. For example, if a mother told her son to help his younger brother and he complied, he would also be *offering help*. To avoid this, *compliance* was not included as one of the twelve categories of social interaction but treated separately.

Thus, although the fieldworkers and coders attempted to follow the conceptual system set down in the *Field Guide*, many modifications had to be made. The resulting system, though far from perfect,

Table 14. The frequency of the twelve acts by culture and for the pooled sample.

Act	Nyan-songo (Kenya)	Juxtla-huaca (Mexico)	Tarong (Philippines)	Taira (Japan)	Khala-pur (India)	Orchard Town (New England)	Total
Acts sociably	274	432	971	324	236	558	2795
Insults	159	96	451	205	104	133	1148
Offers help	156	148	280	97	60	86	827
Reprimands	222	64	185	112	67	102	752
Offers support	106	110	251	73	33	37	610
Seeks dominance	29	71	123	133	128	125	609
Seeks help	28	91	127	87	122	148	603
Seeks attention	62	69	100	89	57	226	603
Suggests responsibly	171	93	138	69	47	38	556
Assaults sociably	48	52	237	95	38	59	529
Touches	21	78	136	17	19	15	286
Assaults	66	45	45	50	36	21	263
Totals	1342	1349	3044	1351	947	1548	9581

represents a step forward, both practically and theoretically, toward a general taxonomy of social behavior.*

Table 14 shows the frequency of the twelve acts by culture. It varies from 2,795 acts for *acts sociably* to 263 for *assaults*. These raw frequencies were converted for each child into two scores for each of the twelve act types. One was a rate score, which was the frequency for a given act type divided by the number of minutes of observation. The other was a *proportion score*, which was the frequency for an act type divided by the total acts of all twelve types performed by a given child. There was considerable variation in the overall rate of

*This taxonomy has been further revised and tested in Kenya. A methodological report on the revised system is forthcoming (B. Whiting, n.d.).

interaction from culture to culture. Since this could either be a true difference or attributable to the different techniques and skills of observers, proportion scores rather than rate scores will be used in the analyses to be presented in the following chapters.

In sum, standard observational procedures were reasonably well carried out. Setting sampling might have been improved upon. With prescience, the twelve response types finally chosen could have been defined in advance. This might have resulted in greater observer reliability, but the inductive method followed had the advantage of insuring that the response types were meaningful in all six cultures.

the raw frequencies (in the chart on p. 64) were converted for each child into two scores for each of the twelve act types:

① RATE SCORE → The frequency for a given act type ÷ by the # of minutes of observation

② PROPORTION SCORE → The frequency for an act type ÷ by the total acts of all 12 types performed by a given child.

there was considerable variation in the overall rate interaction from culture to culture. Since this could be either a true difference or attributable to the different techniques + skills of observers, proportion scores rather than rate scores will be used in the analyses

65

4 The Effect of Culture on the Social Behavior of Children

Cultural features such as the economy, social structure, settlement pattern, and household and family organization presumably determine the learning environments in which children are brought up, thus influencing their behavior. The children of our six diverse cultures accordingly exhibited distinct patterns of social behavior. Our concern, however, is not with the unique features of each culture or group of children. Instead, we will attempt to distinguish the similarities and contrasts among the six cultures to determine whether or not they correspond to similarities and contrasts in the children's patterns of social behavior.

If culture had no effect upon the social behavior of children the relative frequencies of the twelve behavior types should be the same or very similar in all six cultures. Table 15 shows that this is not true. Although *acts sociably* ranks highest in all six cultures, there is considerable variation in the rank ordering of the other types. To attempt to explain the rank order differences for each behavior type

[handwritten margin notes:]
Their concern is NOT w/the unique feature of each culture or group of children. Instead, we'll attempt to distingu. The similarities + contrasts among the 6 cultures to determine whether or not they correspond to Sims. & contrast in the children's patterns of social behavior.

66

Table 15. Rank order of the frequency of the twelve acts by culture and for total sample.

Act	Nyan-songo (africa)	Juxtla-huaca (Mexico)	Tarong (Phillipines)	Taira (Japan)	Khala-pur (N. India)	Orchard Town (New England)	Total
Acts sociably	1	1	1	1	1	1	1
Insults	4	5	2	2	4	4	2
Offers help	5	2	3	5	6	7	3
Reprimands	2	10	6	4	5	6	4
Seeks dominance	10	8	10	3	2	5	5
Seeks help	11	6	9	9	3	3	6
Suggests responsibly	3	4	7	8	8	9	7
Offers support	6	3	4	10	11	10	8.5
Seeks attention	8	9	11	7	7	2	8.5
Assaults sociably	9	11	5	6	9	8	10
Touches	12	7	8	12	12	12	11.5
Assaults	7	12	12	11	10	11	11.5

would be difficult, if not impossible. It is unlikely, however, that each of the twelve behaviors is independent. More probably some pairs of behaviors have similar functions and are positively correlated with one another, while other pairs have contrasting functions and are negatively correlated. If there actually are underlying dimensions that produce such functional clustering of behaviors, and if these dimensions can be discovered and described, our task will be greatly simplified.)

In our initial attempts to discover whether or not there was an interpretable structure among the twelve behaviors we used the individual scores over the total sample of 134 children. The results of both a factor analysis (Longabaugh, 1966) and MDSAL multidimensional scaling (Whiting and Whiting, 1973) have been previously published. These strategies permitted variation due to individual differences among children within each culture, as well as differences due to cultural membership. Since it is our purpose here to determine what structure could be attributed to culture alone, it is more appropriate to pool the children's scores for each culture. The median proportion score on each of the behaviors was calculated for each culture. This averaged out individual differences and gave values that could be attributed to culture alone. These scores were then intercorrelated to provide a 12 × 12 matrix, and a MDSAL scaling procedure (Kruskal, 1964) was carried out in both three and two dimensions.* Since the latter was simple, interpretable, and had a stress value of .087 (which is considered acceptable), it was chosen for the analysis which follows.

As can be seen from Figure 13, *offers help, offers support,* and *suggests responsibly* have high positive values on the vertical axis (Dimension A)†, while *seeks help, seeks dominance,* and *seeks attention* have high negative values. Dimension A thus contrasts nurturance (*offers help* and *offers support*) and responsibility (*suggests responsibly*) with dependence (*seeks help* and *seeks attention*) and dominance (*seeks dominance*).

In a similar manner *acts sociably, assaults sociably,* and *touches*‡

---

*This procedure was suggested by Michael Burton as a more appropriate procedure than factor analysis for the type of data with which we were dealing. For a description of the assumptions and uses of MDSAL scaling procedures see Shepard, Romney, and Nerlove (1972).

†For heuristic reasons Figure 13 was rotated 90° counterclockwise. Dimension A was the horizontal axis resulting from the MDSAL procedure.

‡*Touches* also has a high positive value on the vertical axis and could have been assigned to the nurturant-responsible polar cluster. However, since physical contact seemed more relevant to friendliness, sociability, and intimacy than to nurturance and responsibility, it was assigned arbitrarily to Dimension B.

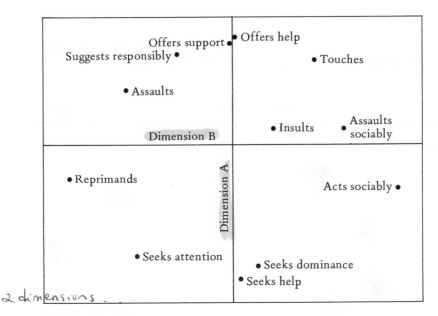

Figure 13. Multidimensional scaling (MDSAL) of cultural medians for the twelve types of social behavior.

have relatively high positive values on the horizontal axis (Dimension B), while *reprimands* and *assaults* have relatively high negative values on it. This second dimension contrasts sociable-intimate behavior with authoritarian-aggressive behavior. It should be noted that *insults* does not have high values on either dimension; it, therefore, is not considered a defining attribute and will not be considered in the analysis to follow.

The scaling procedure indicates that there are indeed redundancies in the data and the scores for the twelve behaviors can be reduced to two scores, one for each dimension.

The next step in the analysis was to calculate a score on Dimension A and Dimension B for each culture. To do this, a value on each dimension had to be assigned to each child in the sample. To avoid exaggerating the effect of those with low mean scores, the scores for each behavior type were standardized over the whole sample. This resulted in a set of individual child scores for each behavior that had a mean of zero and a standard deviation of one. These standard scores were summed in the following manner to give three new child scores for each dimension: (1) nurturance-responsibility polar cluster score = offers help + offers support + suggests responsibly; (2) dependence-dominance polar cluster score = seeks help + seeks attention + seeks dominance; (3) Dimension A score = (1) – (2).

Scores for Dimension B were calculated in a similar manner: (1) sociable-intimate polar cluster score = acts sociably + assaults sociably + touches; (2) authoritarian-aggressive polar cluster score = reprimands + assaults; (3) Dimension B score = (1) – (2). If our choice of indices for the two dimensions are appropriate, Dimension A and Dimension B should be approximately independent—the correlation between them should approach zero. Since the actual correlation was –.05, this requirement was reasonably met.

DIMENSION A AND CULTURAL COMPLEXITY

The median scores for the children in each culture on Dimension A are given in Table 16. Nyansongo, Juxtlahuaca, and Tarong all have positive scores. Children in these cultures were on the average more nurturant and responsible than dependent and dominant. The mean scores for Taira, Orchard Town, and Khalapur were negative. Children in these cultures were on the average more dependent and dominant than nurturant and responsible.

According to the model adopted for this study, there should be

Table 16. Medians for the children of each culture on Dimension A (based on proportion scores for each child standardized over the whole sample).

Khalapur *n. India*	Orchard Town	Taira *Japan*	Tarong	Juxtla-huaca	Nyansongo
−1.04	−0.75	−0.24	+0.48	+0.54	+1.14
Dependent-dominant				Nurturant-responsible	

some contrast in the maintenance systems—for example, the social, economic, and political structures—of the two sets of cultures that impels parents to press children toward being nurturant-responsible on the one hand or dependent-dominant on the other. It is not assumed that parents do so in any conscious way, though this might be the case in some instances, but rather that different daily life routines dictated by different sets of environmental and historical factors impel parents to interact with children in different ways, to assign different tasks, and to reward and punish different ways of behaving. It is also true that the methods of socialization adopted by different cultures prepare the children for the adult roles that they must assume when they grow up.

Cultural complexity suggests itself as the variable that differentiates the behavior of children on Dimension A. Simpler societies, lacking superordinate authority (B. Whiting, 1950; Swanson, 1960), require a high degree of cooperation within the family, the extended family, the lineage, or the micro-community. Complex societies, on the other hand, with a multiplicity of roles and a hierarchical structure should train their children to be competitive and achievement-oriented. Egoistic-dominance and attention-seeking is consonant with such training. Even to seek help to gain one's ends is not incompatible with a hierarchical system.

Recent cross-cultural research (Tatje and Naroll, 1970; Murdock, 1973) has identified a number of features that have been used to construct scales to determine cultural complexity. Items in these scales include occupational specialization, a cash economy, a nucleated settlement pattern, a centralized political and legal system, and a priesthood. These will be considered in testing the hypothesis that cultural complexity is a determinant of children's scores on Dimension A.

Orchard Town. Orchard Town, whose children have the most egoistic scores, fulfills all the criteria of complexity. None of the fathers in the sample were engaged in subsistence farming; all were salaried employees in a large variety of businesses and professions or were self-employed entrepreneurs. The culture of New England includes the whole spectrum of specialized occupations. Subsistence farming was absent; marketing and exchange were based on cash. The settlement pattern of Orchard Town was nucleated. It had a school, a firehouse, two churches, a library, a gas station, a railroad station, and a women's club, as well as numerous stores and shops. Yankee culture is characterized by a social class system, a federal court, and a complex and centralized political system. The families in the sample belonged to a Baptist church, which supported a full-time minister and espoused a belief in a high and moral god (Fischer and Fischer, 1963).

Khalapur. The children of Khalapur have the second highest scores on the egoistic side of Dimension A. Since all the fathers in the Khalapur sample owned their own agricultural land and lived from its produce, specialized occupations were not represented (Hitchcock and Minturn, 1963). These Rajput families, however, were by no means self-sufficient but were enmeshed in a complex system of

economic interdependence involving a high degree of specialization.
"Each Rajput family is dependent for services on families belonging
to nine other caste groups, and these families in turn are dependent
on the Rajput families they serve for most of their food. Water carriers and sweepers come to a Rajput house every day . . . Every
family in addition is served by a carpenter, blacksmith, barber, potter,
washerman, and leatherworker." (Minturn and Hitchcock, 1963, p.
223.) Although these services were usually paid for in food, there was
a monetary system, and some food, clothing, and other goods were
exchanged for cash. Like Orchard Town, Khalapur was a nucleated
town containing buildings other than dwellings and their attached
outhouses. There was a temple, a high school, a cooperative seed
store, a brick kiln, and a sugar mill, as well as numerous small shops.
Social stratification was represented by the caste system. The Brahmin caste provided a specialized priesthood. Although some of the
priests supplemented their income by farming, most made a living
by carrying out their professional duties.

Taira. The culture of Taira, whose children are also on the egoistic
side of Dimension A, was less complex than either Orchard Town or
Khalapur but still falls on the complex side of the ledger. Most of the
adult males were subsistence farmers, but there were a number of
salaried artisans, clerks, and professionals, including carpenters, a rice
miller, a storekeeper, several store clerks, a doctor, a schoolteacher,
and a postmaster (Maretzki and Maretzki, 1963). Since only fifteen
out of twenty-four families grew enough rice to be self-sufficient, a
cash income was required to supplement this staple of their diet, as
well as to purchase ready-made clothes, building materials such as
wood, tiles, and cement, tobacco, alcoholic beverages, sweets, toilet
articles, some medical supplies, and other luxuries. Farmers bought

their tools, students their books and written materials. Finally, cash was needed to pay taxes. This cash income was obtained by most unsalaried families through lumbering. A few families had a cash surplus of rice or sweet potatoes and some raised and sold pigs. Several fishermen sold their catch in the village, and a few families raised silkworms and tea as cash crops.

Taira, like Khalapur and Orchard Town, contained numerous specialized buildings. There was a township office, a village office, a post office, a store, a dispensary, a warehouse, a rice mill, a firehouse, a police station, a prayer house, and a shrine. Political authority beyond the level of the local community was vested in a system imposed originally by the Japanese and modified by the Americans during their occupation of Okinawa following World War II. It consisted of township officials, who were responsible to district officials, who were in turn responsible to the central Ryukyuan government. There were at each level various functional departments such as those concerned with education, finance, industry, agriculture, health, and sanitation. Effective centralized political authority was present before the establishment of the Japanese administrative system, when Okinawa was governed by men who levied taxes throughout the island and held political control over the villages.

note

With the exception of the families of the fishermen, who were looked down upon somewhat, there was little or no class stratification in Taira at the time of the study. This was not always so for "between 1875 and 1895, when the court life at the old capital of Shuri was broken up under Japanese influence, many families of noble origin moved into the country to become farmers . . . The noble families who settled in the valleys and hills preserved their distinctive traditions until the end of World War II. Their noble descent was noted in the population register and intermarriage with commoners was discouraged." (Maretzki and Maretzki, 1963, p. 373.)

Whether the Okinawan "priestess" should qualify as such or be classed as a female shaman is difficult to say. According to Maretzki and Maretzki (1963, p. 377), she "participates in daily work like the rest of the women in the village. Only when performing services outside the community is the priestess paid a small fee. Within the village she receives the food and *sake* which are offered in the ceremony. From this account it does not seem that Okinawan culture can claim a true priesthood.

Tarong. Tarong, whose children scored on the nurturant side of Dimension A, was simpler than any of the cultures described above. Owing to a long occupation, first by the Spanish and then by Americans, before the Philippines became an independent nation, the national culture is modern and complex. For the purposes of this analysis, however, the culture of the Ilocos of northern Luzon rather than the national culture is relevant. Since the politically dominant group speaks a different language, Tagalog, and Manila, the capital, is three hundred miles distant, the Ilocos have been rather slow to acculturate and have retained most of their aboriginal customs. Although a Christian church had been established in the province by 1560, a report, probably written in 1594, indicates that "the province . . . is . . . poorly populated by Spaniards. It contains many churches and Christians, and all the people are not wholly Christian because of the lack of ministers" (Nydegger and Nydegger, 1963, p. 699). The Nydeggers go on to say: "later observations and records indicate the Spanish population continued to be relatively low while, if the present belief systems may be accepted as an index, a scarcity of ministers continues" (p. 700).

The Ilocos aboriginally were subsistence farmers, and they were at the time of the study. Whereas only a little over 10 percent of the Tairan families grew enough rice to be self-sufficient, 40 percent of the families in Tarong did so. Most of the remaining family heads were primarily farmers who supplemented their income by working as farmhands during the harvesting season or as part-time carpenters, traders, basketmakers, ropemakers, veterinarians, and so on. Women supplemented the family income by engaging in trade, weaving, or acting as seamstresses; almost all these occupations were part-time. "Only some carpenters and few traders can be said to make a living from their specialities. . . . Tarongans are largely but not completely self-sufficient. Salt, some fish, coconuts and betel are the only food stuffs regularly imported. The most costly necessary imports consist of iron tools and machines such as knives, chisels, scissors, pressure lamps, sewing machines and so on. Thread and ready-made cloth, pottery, soap, and jewelry are not manufactured in Tarong and require cash outlay." (Ibid., pp. 731, 732.)

Tarong, the Ilocano settlement from which the sample of children was drawn (see Figure 3), consisted of five contiguous hamlets, the largest consisting of eighteen households, the smallest of three. There was but one specialized building—a schoolhouse—within its boundaries. Specialized buildings situated at the district capital, five miles away, consisted of a large church, a municipal hall, and numerous shops and markets.

Only since 1948, when the Philippines became independent, have the Ilocanos participated in a political organization with indigenous centralized authority. Although power was centralized both under the Spaniards and later under the Americans, it was foreign and accepted reluctantly by Tarongans. Even today, "the *sitio* (hamlet) is, in fact, the effective functioning unit politically as well as socially" (ibid., p. 756). Except for capital crimes, which were rare, almost all conflicts were handled by informal means at the local level. If these informal techniques failed, the case was brought before the district (población) justice of the peace, a step not taken lightly for it involved litigation and expenses usually greater than the disagreement merited. Only two Tarongan cases in three years reached the justice of the peace.

Measured by landholdings, there was a considerable difference in the wealth of the families of Tarong, but this did not seem to have consolidated into a class system. The families that had to rent additional acreage were considered luckier than the nearly landless tenant farmers but they did not have higher social status. A few of the wealthy landlords who did not themselves work their land could be considered to constitute a superior class. Since few of these landlords were Tarongans and all of them lived in the provincial capital, these class distinctions were not very salient in the life of a Tarongan child.

Aboriginally, and at the time of the study, the most important mediator between the Tarongan and the spirit world was a shaman or medicine man. Since it was believed that death and disease were caused by spirits, these shamans were usually called upon as curers in the cases of illness. They did not charge enough for their services to support themselves and were not organized into any semblance of a priesthood. Tarongans, however, were nominally Christian and thus involved with the Catholic priesthood. Their contact with the church, which was miles distant, was limited to baptisms, weddings, and funerals. Few Tarongans ever attended mass. In the daily lives of the people Catholicism cannot be said to compete in importance with the concern for ancestors and other spirits.

Juxtlahuaca. The Mixtecans of Juxtlahuaca, whose children scored on the nurturant-responsible end of Dimension A, like the Ilocanos were subsistence farmers. Descendants of a people conquered by the Spaniards in the sixteenth century and isolated from both Oaxaca, the state capital, (and) Mexico City, they have retained most of their aboriginal culture. "Although priests penetrated the area early in introducing religious changes, the basic subsistence patterns have been little affected. The addition of some fruits and vegetables was supplementary: maize, beans and chile have remained the basic diet. Even the introduction of oxen and the plow have failed to affect greatly the pattern of land exploitation. Thus the intrusion of Spanish culture elements in the Mixtec area has involved little change in such features as land usage, subsistence patterns, residence, and certain aspects of village organization." (Romney and Romney, 1963, p. 546.)

The Mixtecans who were the subjects of this study lived in a barrio or ward of the town of Juxtlahuaca. Except for this barrio, where the Mixtec language was spoken and native dress worn, the town was occupied by ladinos, Spanish-speaking Mexicans. "All the men in the barrio, save one, earn their primary living through the cultivation of maize" (ibid., p. 574). "Wage work within the barrio is unknown, but barrio men sometimes do farmwork for townspeople, even though wages are extremely low. Better pay can be earned in Tlaxiaco, in the mines, or in the sugar refinery at Atencingo, Puebla. Several men, or occasionally a whole family, will go there to live and work for a period of weeks or months. Half a dozen men have been as far as the United States as *braceros* for six months or more. . . . Several men have part-time specialties which provide them with additional income. One man carves wooden masks worn during the religious drama performed at the fiesta of the patron saint. Another bakes the bread

78

milpa = maize fields

served during this fiesta. . . . Several men serve as butchers at the fiesta and are paid in food. One man with grown sons still at home leaves them in charge of the *milpa* (maize fields) and makes regular trips to Copala to sell corn which he has bought for this purpose. The young men of another family work as carpenters in el Centro (the Spanish-speaking part of town). Several others make or lay adobe or tile which they sell in the barrio and in town." (Ibid., pp. 577–578.)

el Centro

Most of the women engaged in part-time specialties to supplement the family income. These included making and selling tortillas, marketing garden produce, embroidering and making clothing on order for the ladinos of el Centro. A few of the young girls leave the village for extended periods to work as servants in Oaxaca or Mexico City. Specialized occupations were thus part-time and, compared to the value of the food produced and consumed, the cash income of a family was small. Cash income was needed to buy tools, utensils, and some clothing, to pay taxes, and primarily to pay for food, cigarettes, liquor, and the other things used for ceremonies on the occasion of the marriage, birth, or death of a family member.

Although the town of Juxtlahuaca contained a church, several municipal buildings, an open-air market, several shops and stores, a telegraph office, and two schools, there was but one specialized building, a church, in the barrio, which was otherwise entirely resi-dential. Furthermore, the barrio was clearly separated from el Centro by a deep gorge through which a stream ran, and perhaps even more separated by a language barrier. The settlement pattern of the barrio was similar to Mixtecan hamlets in the hinterlands which are not attached to Mexican villages, in that both consist of a group of dwellings with no buildings except for a church and a community building for specialized functions.

note

key pt.

Political authority was very similar to that of the Ilocanos. The Mixtecans were subject to the Mexican national government with its various departments, but their actual contact with it was minimal. Even though Mexico has been an independent nation for a long time, the people of the barrio continued to speak Mixtecan as their first language rather than Spanish, indicating that their primary cultural identity was Indian rather than Mexican. As a consequence, conflicts between members of the barrio were settled within the barrio by informal means. "It is rare for a conflict between members of the barrio to reach the Mexican court systems" (ibid., p. 607).

Although there was a Catholic church in the barrio with a full-time priest, the important focus of Mixtecan religion was the cofradía system. A cofradía consists of a group of people organized for the purpose of honoring a specific saint through celebrations. The officers of a cofradía consisted of a mayordomo and diputados, who, although they were intensely involved both financially and in terms of time and effort in the preparation for and the carrying out of the ceremony, were in no sense religious specialists. Any adult male who had accumulated sufficient wealth was expected to sponsor a ceremony as a mayordomo. Furthermore, his duties ceased with the end of the ceremony. The cofradía system effectively prevented the development of a class system based on wealth. The Romneys reported that one fiesta cost the mayordomo 1,500 pesos, the helpers 250 pesos each. (Ibid., p. 606.)

Nyansongo. The Gusii of Nyansongo were also primarily subsistence farmers. Except for a few women who engaged part-time in market-ing, there were no specialized occupations in the community. The family income might be supplemented by wages from the labor of some of its adult male members or by the sale of surplus crops or the harvest of small holdings of cash crops such as tea or coffee. Like the Ilocanos and Mixtecans, this cash was used for paying taxes and school fees and buying tools, utensils, clothing, and condiments.

In Nyansongo, whose children are more nurturant than those of any of the other five cultures a man's wealth was measured not in shillings but in the ownership of cattle. Since cattle were the medium of exchange for the payment of bride price, which was large enough to cause a redistribution of the herds at each generation, the bride price, like the Mixtecan cofradía system, prevented the development of social classes. To quote LeVine and Lloyd (1963, p. 29), "Thus in Nyansongo . . . there are only one or two wealthy men who are the acknowledged leaders and whose opinions on local affairs are granted extraordinary weight. Although there is open recognition of economic inequality, there are no social classes among the Gusii."

All the buildings in the community were either dwellings, bachelor huts, or granaries. Keumbu, a shopping and administrative center for Nyansongo, was less than a quarter-mile distant and Kisii, the district capital, was eight miles away.

"Located at Keumbu are the chief's office, a tribal police head-quarters, the local assembly hall, a prison cubicle, and the official chief's residence. . . . There is a Roman Catholic primary and inter-mediate day school where 400 students are taught by Gusii teachers. On the other side of a dirt road from the chief's office and school, there is a market, a neat rectangle of Gusii shops, and a restaurant." (Ibid., p. 23.) At the time of this study, even though British authority had been in effect for nearly fifty years, "many features of the indigenous authority system could still be observed in operation. The seven tribes of Gusiiland were converted into seven administrative 'locations' each with its own chief. The chiefs are appointed by the

Provincial Commissioner, but are chosen only from among the descended clans of the tribes they are to govern. Each chief has under him a number of 'subheadmen' who used to function only in their own clan territories but were recently given multiclan territories in an action designed to reduce clan parochialism." (Ibid., p. 89.)

Sorcerers and diviners were the only religious specialists in Gusii culture. Part-time practitioners, they were not organized into anything approaching a priesthood.

Summary. If the six cultures are rated on each of the dimensions of complexity discussed above—degree of occupational specialization, differentiation of settlement pattern, political centralization, social stratification, and religious specialization—two culture types appear: simple—Nyansongo, Juxtlahuaca, and Tarong, which scored low on each of these dimensions; and complex—Orchard Town, Khalapur, and Taira, which scored high. This division into two types on the basis of complexity corresponds to their scores on Dimension A. As indicated in Table 16, the three simpler societies all scored on the nurturant-responsible side of the dimension: Nyansongo (+1.14), Juxtlahuaca (+0.54), and Tarong (+0.48), while the more complex are on the dependent-dominant end: Taira (–0.24), Orchard Town (–0.75), and Khalapur (–1.04).

Learning Environments

This finding, although interesting, does not specify the mechanism by which the complexity of a culture influences the social behavior of children. An analysis of the daily routines of the children in each of the six cultures should illuminate this problem. If different tasks are assigned and different settings prescribed to children in cultures with varying degrees of cultural complexity, the mechanism by which a structural feature of the culture influences the social behavior of children might be discovered.

One of the most obvious differences between simple and complex societies is found in the nature of the tasks assigned to children, the work they are expected to perform. What are the factors which lead to these differences? Analysis of the data suggests that the mother's workload is an important variable; mothers in simple societies have more to do than mothers in more complex societies.

Women in all six societies were responsible for the care of children, preparing food, cooking for the family, and keeping the house clean. Variations in the amount of time and energy required of them depends in large part on the number of specialized agencies in the society. If there is a town water supply, specialists who manufacture and distribute fuel, specialists who process grain, and kindergartens and schools to care for children during the day, then women's housekeeping and child-tending responsibilities are less arduous and time-consuming. Similarly, in more specialized societies women have fewer agricultural responsibilities and, until they enter the industrial labor market, fewer additional activities outside the home. In subsistence agricultural societies, where the gardens are near home and there are no plows or tractors or draft animals, women are usually important contributors and may spend up to four or five hours a day in the gardens, the men delegating to them, as among the Nyansongo, the hoeing of the soil and the weeding of the food crops. As in the other societies, these women were also responsible for cooking and for the care of children. In such societies the women organize the children to help; the greater the workload the more they will delegate to them. If being involved in the maintenance of the family well-being is training in responsibility, the children who perform the chores

83

should be more responsible than those who do not. If serving as caretakers for younger siblings is training in nurturance, children who help care for infant siblings should be more nurturant than those who do not.

Table 17 summarizes the percentage of children who performed various types of chores. It will be noted that Orchard Town families have the fewest potential chores; the Juxtlahuancans, Tarongans, and Nyansongans the most. The percentages of children in each society assigned each task are based on the reports of the mothers (see Min-

Table 17. Percentage of children in each culture reported and/or observed performing certain chores and tasks.

Chore or task	Simpler cultures			Complex cultures		
	Nyan-songo	Juxtla-huaca	Tarong	Taira	Khala-pur	Orchard Town
Collecting firewood	44	27	58	13	13	—
Fetching water	75	64	20	18	29	—
Collecting fodder	0	5	13	8	17	—
Cleaning and sweeping	31	41	59	59	33	92
Preparing food	19	5	42	0	4	0
Harvesting vegetables	25	14	36	0	9	0
Grinding grain	38	9	8	0	0	—
Cooking	31	5	29	0	0	4
Gardening	75	14	13	13	4	—
Tending fowl	0	9	29	25	—	13
Tending house-hold animals	0	23	33	21	13	—
Tethering	0	9	29	0	0	—
Herding	50	5	37	4	33	—

turn and Lambert, 1964, ch. 6) and the observations of the children, and should be considered estimates. The mothers were asked what work they expected of their children, an open-ended question with no probes for specific chores. In the observations no attempt was made to sample settings so as to assess the children's workload; occasionally however, they were found performing chores. The six cultures fall in an almost identical rank order by these two independent measures of economic tasks.

In all societies children were asked to run errands, their parents commanding them to fetch and carry, and, where there were no telephones, directing them to carry messages to neighboring houses. Most adults were unaware of how frequently they made use of the children for these purposes. As a mother or grandmother worked, she would command her child to bring her a bowl or a pan, fetch a stick of wood, call a sibling, go next door and borrow an ember to start the fire, or go to the store and make a small purchase. When a child has had frequent experience performing an act at his or her mother's request, the mother may decide that she can now require the child to do the work without detailed instruction or constant supervision. We classify work done under such conditions as tasks or chores. One of the first errands which becomes a chore is carrying firewood.

With the exception of Orchard Town, women in all the societies cooked over small, open fires and hence required fuel daily. Wherever it was practical, children were requested to help keep the house supplied with fuel. In Nyansongo, Juxtlahuaca, and Tarong children performed this chore more frequently than in Khalapur and Taira, where parents needed less help. In Khalapur, dung cakes—the majority made by lower-caste servants—were used, and children were asked to pile or carry them; in Taira many of the families are engaged in lumbering and selling firewood, and it was most convenient for the men and women to bring the household supply on their way back from the mountain. Children contributed most in Tarong and Nyansongo, where they not only piled and carried wood but also collected it. Wood for the Mixtecan households came primarily from the mountainsides and was brought down on burros. Except for the older boys, children just stacked the wood in the yard and brought it into the cook shack. In sum, Nyansongo and Tarong parents utilized their young children most frequently for this task and required harder work, expecting children to collect wood on the noncultivated land surrounding the homesteads and hamlets.

In five societies there was no water piped to the houses; hence the daily supply of water had to be carried. The age at which children began to help and the amount of water they were able to carry depended on the distance of the supply from the house, the ease of access and safety of the water hole or well, and the type of container used. The Nyansongo children, who contributed most frequently to the supply, fetched water from shallow rivers. Although some of the paths to the homestead were steep, none were as precipitous as the paths to the water holes in Tarong, which is reflected in the lower contribution of Tarong children. Next to Nyansongo, the Juxtlahuaca families had the largest number of children carrying water, but the task was not arduous. There were wells in many barrio courtyards, so water did not have to be carried far. Furthermore, the wells were constructed so as to be quite safe. In Khalapur family servants brought water to the house, but children carried it around the court-yard and drew it from the household well. When it was necessary to supplement the supply, only older children were sent to the town well, perhaps because it is more dangerous and further from home. In

Taira the two village water tanks were easily accessible, but large pails were used and carried on poles shouldered by two people—a task which required more physical strength than carrying a small contain- *— interesting* er. In sum, more Nyansongo and Juxtlahuacan children carried water than in the other three societies, with the Nyansongo children having a much longer haul than the Juxtlahuacan children.

Housecleaning is another universal chore, and the percentages reflect the complexity of the houses and household furnishings. *— interesting* Orchard Town had the most elaborate houses requiring the most care. Almost all the mothers of this society expected their children to help with the dishes, set the table, empty the trash, and tidy their rooms. Some even expected heavy housecleaning on weekends. Houses in Khalapur, Tarong, and Taira were the next most elaborate, and 59 percent of the Tarongan and Tairan children did housework. Tarongan children polished floors, washed dishes, and swept the yard; Tairan children mopped floors and cleaned lamps. In Khalapur the women not only had fewer economic chores to perform because they were confined to the courtyards, but they also had servants who helped sweep and clean, which probably explains why they made less use of child labor. Juxtlahuacan and Nyansongo houses required less care. Juxtlahuacan houses were used primarily for sleeping, storage, and entertaining visitors. Cooking took place in a separate shack and much of the daily living took place in the patio. Girls helped wash dishes and pans and both boys and girls helped care for the sleeping mats and beds and swept, boys often being assigned the task of sweeping the patio. The Nyansongo had very simple mud and wattle houses with a few wooden benches and chairs. Children washed the pots and cups and swept the earthen floor—all the housecleaning required. In sum, the use of children for housecleaning varied with the elaborate-

Carrying water, Taira

ness of the house and furnishings; it was greatest in Orchard Town and least in Nyansongo, where houses were simple and their maintenance not arduous.

The tending of fowl is a casual affair unless the birds are kept caged as in Taira and Orchard Town. In Tarong, Juxtlahuaca, and Nyansongo chickens wandered around and the only care was to throw them grain occasionally or shoo them out of the house and away from food. Of the two societies that caged the birds the Tairan boys had a more time-consuming job than the Orchard Town boys, since rather than feeding the fowl grain purchased at the store, they cut grass and gathered other feed.

The care of large animals required more time and effort. It is, moreover, necessary to distinguish between animals kept around the house (whether penned, tethered, or just wandering around the courtyard, as pigs do in Juxtlahuaca) and those which are herded and driven to unfenced pasturage. Chores related to the former type of animal husbandry require less responsibility and are less time consuming than the latter. Table 17 shows the percentage of children responsible for the care of household pigs, goats, and sheep. Only in Tarong were an appreciable number involved with the care of such animals. Children were asked to change the tethering posts of the family goats and were often expected to prepare the pig food. Four of the Juxtlahuacan children both cut fodder and fed the unpenned pigs. In Taira, like fowl, animals were penned and food was collected and fed by the children. Khalapur families had no pigs or sheep or goats. Boys might carry fodder to the cattle or herd them in unfenced pastures. In Nyansongo sheep and goats were herded with the cattle.

One of the most responsible tasks which could be assigned to children was the care of large animals which were pastured in un-

fenced land, particularly when such land abutted on gardens and
fields of grain. Included in this category are animals which are
tethered but must be driven from area to area and taken to the well
or river to be watered. The Nyansongo had the largest number of
children (50 percent) involved in the herding of animals. The young
boys took the cattle, sheep, and goats to the homestead pastures or
drove them along the sides of the road where there was grass. They
were responsible for seeing that the animals did not get into the
gardens and ruin their own or someone else's food supply. They
drove the cattle, sheep, and goats to the river to drink and took care
that they returned home with the proper number of animals.
Although the percentage figures suggest that Tarongan children were
as involved as Khalapur children (37 as opposed to 33 percent), the
children of Tarong spent less time with the cattle than did the
Khalapur herd boys. The Tarongan families had one or two carabao
which were tethered when not being used as draft animals and when
not being driven to the well twice a day to be watered. The boys in
our sample managed these large animals when they changed the tether
posts, sometimes letting them graze untethered for short periods.
Some of the boys drove or rode the caraboa to the well, others
accompanied and helped their fathers. In Khalapur the herd boy had
more animals to manage, drove them longer distances, and, like
Nyansongo boys, pastured them in unfenced fields where, if not
properly supervised, they could stray into the cultivated fields and
ruin the crops.

Although numerous families in Juxtlahuaca had sheep, only one
family in our sample had a flock and their son herded the sheep on
Saturdays and Sundays when he was not in school. Another boy in
the sample had several burros to take care of. In Taira one boy
helped care for the family horse.

Leveling a new paddy with carabao, Tarong

philippines

In sum, herd boys in Khalapur and Nyansongo, especially if they
did not attend school, might spend as much as four hours a day caring
for cattle and, in Nyansongo, sheep and goats. The herd boy might
play with other boys while he tended the animals, and might seem to
have an easy existence, but he was held responsible for any damage
either to the animals or to the crops, and could expect a severe beat-
ing for any negligence. Tarongan boys learned to manage the carabao
but spent less time with the animals.

Two types of chores were rarely assigned to children in the 3–10
age group. The first is cooking, which is generally done by older
children. Table 17 shows that almost a third of the Nyansongo children were reported or observed cooking during the study: boiling
maize and beans or roasting potatoes and maize. The Tarongan
children boiled rice. Many more of the children in these societies
helped to prepare food but, in general, the sample children in Orchard
Town, Khalapur, and Taira neither cooked nor helped prepare food
for cooking. Nyansongo girls and boys and Juxtlahuacan and Tarongan girls helped with the tedious work of grinding maize or pounding
rice.

Few children helped in agricultural work, and most tasks were
assigned to older children. It appears that children under 10 were
useful primarily as burden carriers; Khalapur children carried wheat,
sugar cane, or other produce from the fields; Tarongan children
carried rice bundles. Four girls, 7 or over, one Tairan and three
Tarongan, worked in the rice fields helping to plant and transplant.
It appears that only in maize cultures can children really participate
in cultivation at an early age. Seventy-five percent of the sample
children in Nyansongo weeded or hoed. Although Juxtlahuacans also
raised maize and beans as staple crops, most gardens were distant
from the courtyards, hence the use of young children was rare.

Boys carrying fodder, Khalapur

A greater proportion of children from the simpler cultures were expected to help out on important economic and domestic tasks more than were children from the more complex cultures. Table 17 shows that well over half of the Nyansongo children were reported or observed helping out with the gardening, herding, or fetching water. Almost two-thirds of the children of Juxtlahuaca were expected to fetch water, while over 50 percent of the children of Tarong were expected to fetch firewood. The only chore that engaged more than half the children of the more complex cultures was cleaning and sweeping: Taira 59 percent and Orchard Town 92 percent.

The simpler societies not only assigned more tasks to their children but did so at an earlier age. As can be seen in Table 18, Nyansongo children in the 3–4 age group performed all the five major tasks:

Table 18. Youngest age at which over half the children of a given age group were reported or observed performing a given chore or task.

Chore or task		Simpler cultures			Complex cultures		
		Nyan-songo	Juxtla-huaca	Tarong	Taira	Khala-pur	Orchard Town
Carrying wood and water		3–4	3–4	3–4	7–10	5–6	—
Preparing food		3–4	7–10	3–4	—	3–4	—
Gardening		3–4	7–10	7–10	—	—	—
Cleaning		3–4	5–6	3–4	3–4	5–6	3–4
Taking care of animals		3–4	3–4	5–6	7–10	7–10	—
Number of tasks performed by 3–4-year-olds		5	2	3	1	1	1

carrying wood and water, preparing food, gardening, cleaning, and taking care of animals. In Tarong 3–4-year-olds did three of these major tasks, in Juxtlahuaca, two. By contrast, the three complex societies expected little of children at this young age but cleaning.

One of the most responsible jobs assigned to children and one which seems most obviously related to nurturance and responsibility was the care of younger siblings. In all societies children were expected to do some child-tending. It is difficult to estimate the amount of caretaking required of the different samples, for, again, the mother interviews were not detailed enough and the setting sampling not adequate. There were striking differences, however, in what types of caretaking mothers were willing to delegate, the age at which they considered a child competent, and the amount of supervision considered necessary. Nyansongo mothers entrusted the youngest babies, required the most responsible caretaking, and did the least supervising once the child nurse was trained. When a Nyansongo child, preferably aged 5–8, was designated as nurse for a baby, he or she assumed the job when the infant was approximately two months of age and continued as such until the child could walk securely. Since few of the children were in school at the time of the study, these child nurses were available all day long. They were observed feeding, bathing, and caring for the infants while their mothers worked in nearby gardens or went to the market. Juxtlahuacan girls might have had an equal amount of responsibility but they were not assigned it until they were at least 8; furthermore, they did not care for unweaned children for such long periods of time as did their Nyansongo counterparts. Tairan children were in school at least half the day. When they came home some of the mothers asked them to carry their infant siblings while the mothers

Child nurse, Nyansongo

went to the gardens to gather produce for the evening meal. There were also 5-year-olds who went to kindergarten with siblings strapped to their backs. These Tairan girls who carried infants patted, bounced, and talked to their charges; if these distractions failed to quiet the infants, the caretakers turned to the teacher or returned home to their mothers or grandmothers. Tairan girls were never observed bathing, feeding, or putting infants to bed. The role of the Tarongan nurse is more similar to the Tairan caretaker than to the Nyansongo. Although mothers started training children as young as 3 to entertain, rock, and protect baby brothers and sisters from flies, they supervised the young caretakers. Khalapur girls and boys held babies, entertained them, and occasionally carried them out to the men's sleeping platform.

One question on the mother interviews indicated the value placed on the help given by child nurses. The mothers were asked who had helped them care for the sample child when he or she was an infant (Minturn and Lambert, 1964, ch. 6). Sixty-nine percent of the Nyansongo mothers and 41 percent of the Juxtlahuacan mothers reported having been helped with their infant by a child, and 25 percent of the Tarongan, 21 percent of the Khalapur, and 12 percent of both Orchard Town and Tairan mothers reported the same. This rank order seems to be the best overall measure of the amount of responsibility for infants delegated by the mothers. The three highest ranking societies are those of the simpler cultures who ranked high on the nurturant-responsible end of Dimension A.

These are also the societies in which children were observed interacting with infants most frequently (see Table 19). In the simpler societies 24–25 percent of the sample child's interaction was with infants, as compared with 3.5–9 percent in the more complex societies.

Table 19. Proportion of all acts to all targets that are made to infants.

Sex	Simpler cultures			Complex cultures		
	Nyan-songo	Juxtla-huaca	Tarong	Taira	Khala-pur	Orchard Town
Boys	16	21	23	5	4	1
Girls	34	29	25	8	14	6
Both	25	25	24	6.5	9	3.5

It should be noted that the care of toddlers requires different skills and behaviors on the part of caretakers. Observation of the interaction of children with 2–4-year-old younger siblings indicated that caretakers of these children were comparatively more apt to reprimand, criticize, and punish. These behaviors, as will be discussed later, are more relevant to Dimension B. The children in Taira were most involved in this type of caretaking, the mothers designating them as responsible for supervising the toddlers who tagged along with their older siblings as they played all over the village. Nyansongo mothers seemed to take it for granted that 2- or 3-year-olds could fend for themselves when left unsupervised in the homestead in the company of their older siblings. Khalapur 3-year-olds, once they ventured outside the courtyard, were not supervised by adults but tagged along after the other children. Only in Tarong, Orchard Town, and Juxtlahuaca did there seem to be continued concern that there be an adult or adolescent supervising children. In these societies adults monitored the yards or patios where the children played.

Another way to compare the degree of responsibility and nurturance required of children in the six cultures is to judge the amount

Child nurse, Khalapur

Child nurse, Juxtlahuaca

of time per day or per week spent doing various types of chores and the amount of responsibility required of each child. In assessing the time, one must bear in mind that school attendance cuts down the number of hours a child is able to work for the family. In Orchard Town, Taira, and Tarong, where there was universal elementary education for all school-age children, there was at most an hour in the morning and two to four hours in the afternoon during the weekdays. The Orchard Town mother expected her child to pick up his or her room and perhaps make his or her bed and help at the evening meal. The Tairan and Tarongan mothers expected not only housecleaning and dish-washing but help with hauling wood and water and animal and child care. Of these two societies more children did more chores in Tarong than in Taira (see Table 20). In Juxtlahuaca and Khalapur, where two-thirds or fewer of the children attended school, there was variation in the amount of work required. Some of the Khalapur boys who carried large bundles of fodder, grain, and sugar cane from the fields, and who also helped care for the cattle, worked long and hard. Their brothers who attended school did few chores. Similarly, some of the Juxtlahuacan older girls did the work of adult women.

To estimate the average degree of task involvement for the children

Table 20. Average number of all chores, including infant and child care.

Sex	Simpler cultures			Complex cultures		
	Nyan-songo	Juxtla-huaca	Tarong	Taira	Khala-pur	Orchard Town
Boys	4.3	2.2	2.8	1.3	1.3	0.8
Girls	3.6	1.7	3.4	1.9	1.4	1.1
Both	4.0	1.9	2.9	1.6	1.3	1.0

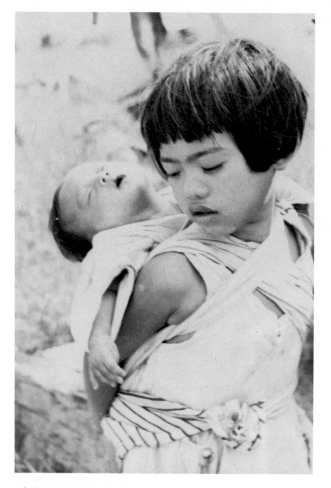

Child nurse, Taira

of each culture their chores were grouped into six types, as follows: (1) carrying wood, water, or fodder; (2) cleaning and other housework; (3) gathering, preparing, or cooking food; (4) gardening; (5) caring for animals (excluding fowl); and (6) caring for younger siblings. The number of different chore types that each child was reported and/or observed to perform was calculated and these scores, averaged for the boys and girls of each culture, are shown in Table 20. As can be seen, Nyansongo children performed the greatest number of different types of tasks, followed by Tarong, Juxtlahuaca, Taira, Khalapur, and Orchard Town. The above ranking of the six cultures, based upon the number of tasks the average child performed, is identical with the ranking on Dimension A.

Both the number and the type of chores expected of the children of a culture are positively related to the cultural evaluation on Dimension A, as measured by the social behavior of the children. It is evident that carrying wood and water, the preparation and cooking of food, gardening, caring for animals, and caring for younger siblings, particularly infants, are more likely to be performed by children of simpler cultures than by children of the more complex societies. It is our interpretation that the performance of these tasks provides one of the mechanisms by which children learn to be nurturant-responsible. All of these chores are intimately related to the daily life of a child aged 3 to 10 and must give him or her a feeling of personal worth and competence.

The importance of chores related to the production and processing of food must be obvious even to a young child; if there is no wood or water the child suffers along with the other members of his or her family. The relation between gardening and eating, too, must be clear. Accompanying an adult to the fields, picking maize, or digging

Gathering water chestnuts, Khalapur

Shelling corn, Nyansongo

potatoes and returning home, cooking, and eating them, is the daily experience of young children in these agricultural societies. Because adults are involved in these activities and it is clear that the mother is busy and needs help, the assignment of chores does not seem arbitrary or unnecessary. Participation must give the child a sense of worth and involvement in the needs of others.

The assignment of infant care implies that the parents can trust their child to be responsible. The care of infants requires constant attention and enough experience to be able both to predict and to change behavior. A child nurse must be able to guess the needs and motivations of his or her small charge and learn what behavior is required to satisfy these needs, the essence of nurturance as we have defined it. The consequences of failure are clear: ignorance or negligence can lead to injury or death.

By contrast, in urban or semi-urban, nonagricultural communities like Orchard Town the tasks assigned to children are less clearly related to the economy and welfare of the child or the child's family and probably seem more arbitrary to the child. Picking up toys or making one's own bed are egoistic, for the benefit of the child. The need for having clothes hung up, bureau drawers tidy, or the bed smoothed out neatly is probably not immediately clear, nor are the consequences of negligence obviously serious. Washing dishes and setting the table are more closely associated with the family as a whole, but the chore may seem less important if the mother uses the respite from work to sit and talk to her husband. Interestingly, housecleaning tasks, of all the chores analyzed, are least related to Dimension A.

Schoolwork is egoistic and competitive. Academic success is individual and, although an educated person may be expected to help his or her family, this is probably not clear to a young Rajput or Tairan school child and was not expected of an Orchard Town child. Rewards for competent school performance and promises for the future are unclear, and the goals must usually seem ever receding to a child. Competition for good grades is training for egoism and does not encourage a child to consider the needs of others.

The differential evaluation of these assigned tasks is reflected in the cultural attitude toward obedience. A series of questions were asked in the mother interviews that could be used to rate a mother's attitude toward obedience: "What happens if __ fails to do his chores?" "Do you expect ___ to obey immediately when you ask him to do something or do you give him a little leeway?" "What if he dawdles or delays?" (Minturn and Lambert, 1964, p. 307).

The scale for measuring the mother's attitude toward obedience in her child which had the highest interjudge reliability (87 percent) was that of the consistency of mother's follow-through of non-routine demands for obedience (ibid., p. 43). The high point on this seven-point scale was "mother always enforces demands and always sees to it that the child performs them." The low point was "mother never enforces demands and pays no attention to whether or not the child complies" (ibid., p. 149). As can be seen from Table 21, an average of 48 percent of the mothers in the simpler cultures claimed that they enforced demands for obedience and consistently followed through, while an average of 29 percent of the mothers in the more complex cultures made equivalent claims.

An estimate of the strength of the mother's response to a challenge to her authority is provided by her answer to the question, "Sometimes children get angry while being criticized or scolded. How do you handle this with ___? What if ___ should kick or strike you?"

Table 21. Differences in mother's control of child's behavior.

Mother's behavior	Simpler cultures			Complex cultures		
	Nyan-songo	Juxtla-huaca	Tarong	Taira	Khala-pur	Orchard Town
Percentage middle or high on consistency of obedience demands[a]	37	63	43	42	20	24
Percentage above mean on punishment for aggression to mother[a]	94	81	82	46	47	43
Rate of mother's instigation to child	3.42	1.76	1.88	0.77	0.93	0.96
Proportion of mother's responses that were *seeks dominance* or *suggests responsibly*	0.51	0.52	0.42	0.39	0.30	0.17

[a]Scores from Minturn and Lambert (1964), pp. 159, 139.

The high point on the scale, constructed to measure the mother's response to aggression directed towards herself, consisted of "mother retaliates with extreme aggression" and the low point "mother never aggresses to child under these conditions, nurtures or distracts" (ibid., pp. 307–308, 137).

As shown in Table 21, most mothers from the simpler societies reported that they would not tolerate aggression toward themselves and would punish the child severely for such behavior. Less than half of the mothers in the more complex societies held this attitude. An example from an interview with a mother of a 5-year old Nyansongo boy shows an attitude typical of the simpler cultures. "I can only cane him if I find him becoming angry and hitting me. If he is near I would get hold of him and cane him, but if he runs away I would refuse him food for a couple of days more and he will learn himself what he had done wrong." (Ibid., p. 322.) The response of an Orchard Town mother of a 10-year-old son illustrates the tolerance toward a challenge to authority characteristic of the more complex culture. "I was telling him to pick up something and he got mad. He said, 'How can I do both things at once?' Maybe after I have blown off, I cool off and he gets things done and everything is alright again." (Ibid., p. 334.)

The response of Khalapur mothers is more similar to that of Orchard Town than to Nyansongo. A typical response to the question is given below.

Q. What do you do when she gets angry with you?

A. I console her and take her in my lap. I say "What is wrong with you? Why are you angry?"

Q. What if she should kick or strike you?

A. A child? Oh no! If the child hits me I will hit her back. (Ibid., p. 336.)

The fact that mothers in the simpler societies are more dictatorial is also suggested by an analysis of their interactions with their children. A rate of instigation for each mother was computed by dividing the number of times she was judged to instigate the sample child by the number of observations in which she was noted as present. Another relevant score could be derived from those interacts in which the mother was the instigator. Of all such acts the proportions that were scored *suggests responsibly or seeks dominance* can be taken as an estimate of the mother's attempts to dominate. Table 21 indicates that the mothers in the simpler societies not only instigated their children more but also told them what to do more frequently than the mothers in the more complex societies.

In the simpler cultures the work assigned to young children is such that negligence may lead to injury to infants and toddlers, the destruction of crops which are the family's food supply, or injury to valuable domestic animals. Mothers in these societies enforced obedience and were more dictatorial.

Returning to our hypothesis that the workload of the mother predicts the number of tasks delegated to children and the value which parents place on nurturant behavior (*offering help* and *offering support*) and responsible behavior (*suggesting responsibly*), we have attempted to rank order the workload of the mothers. Since there is no measure which can be quantified, the rank order is based on the ethnographic descriptions published in the Six Culture Series. Two students asked to judge which women worked hardest ranked Nyansongo women first, Tairan women second, Tarong and Juxtlahuaca either third or fourth, Khalapur fifth, and Orchard Town sixth. Comparing the rank order of the mother's workload with that of her child, it can be seen that Taira is out of order. The Tairan children rank fourth, whereas their mothers rank second. There are several possible explanations for this discrepancy. The rank order of the mother's workload was based on an assessment of her work outside the home. If one takes into consideration cooking, cleaning, and child care, the Tairan women have more help than the Nyansongo, Tarongan, and Juxtlahuacan women. As noted above, there was more

Woman carrying firewood and water pot, Nyansongo

Woman planting seed rice, Tarong

specialization in Taira: the water supply was centralized, rice was processed at a mill, the family made cash by selling lumber and bought goods at the town store. Furthermore, grandmothers were present in half of the households, as compared with 21 percent in Tarong and 5 percent in Juxtlahuaca. These Tairan grandmothers were observed and reported to have helped in infant care and in preparing food for the family. Furthermore, Taira has a kindergarten with a teacher who organized play for preschool children; a mother might send her 5-year-old with an infant sibling strapped on her back to school, while she went off to her garden or to the mountains knowing that an adult would be available in case of trouble (Maretzki and Maretzki, 1963). In 50 percent of the cases a grandmother could be called if the teacher could not manage. This revised estimate of a mother's workload would place Taira in fourth rather than second position and would make the correlation correspond exactly to the children's workload.

Summary. Those results of the multidimensional scaling which distinguished two culture types on the basis of differences in the patterns of the social behavior of children seem justified. Cultural complexity and women's workload are associated with the location of the samples of children on Dimension A: the children of the simpler societies being higher on the nurturant-responsible end of the dimension, the children of the more complex societies being higher on the dependent-dominant end. The mechanism which trains for the nurturant-responsible behaviors is the kind of work expected of children, work essential for the economic welfare of the family, work involved in the care of infants.

DIMENSION B AND HOUSEHOLD STRUCTURE

A new dichotomy

When the cultures are classified on the basis of the children's scores on Dimension B rather than Dimension A (see Table 22), a new dichotomy appears. The children of Juxtlahuaca, Orchard Town, and Tarong fall on the positive, sociable-intimate side of the dimension, while Khalapur, Taira, and Nyansongo fall on the negative, authoritarian-aggressive side. Nyansongo is now grouped with Taira and Khalapur rather than with Juxtlahuaca and Tarong, as was the case for Dimension A. Conversely, Orchard Town is now grouped with Juxtlahuaca and Tarong rather than with Taira and Khalapur. It is evident that some attribute other than cultural complexity is needed to account for this classification.

Whereas the structure of the economic + political domains influences the social beh. of children on Dimension A, it is the structure of the family that is related to their beh. on Dimension B.

Whereas the structure of the economic and political domains influences the social behavior of children on Dimension A, it is the structure of the family that is related to their behavior on Dimension B. In Orchard Town, Juxtlahuaca, and Tarong, whose children have positive scores on Dimension B, the nuclear family was the primary domestic unit, whereas in Taira, Khalapur, and Nyansongo, whose children have negative scores, the patrilineal stem, extended, or poly-gynous family was the primary domestic unit. For convenience the

Table 22. Medians for children of each culture on Dimension B (based on proportion scores for each child standardized over the whole sample).

Nyan-songo	Khala-pur	Taira	Juxtla-huaca	Orchard Town	Tarong
−1.37	−0.46	−0.10	+0.20	+0.41	+0.70
Authoritarian-aggressive				Sociable-intimate	

former will hereinafter be referred to as nuclear family culture and the latter as extended family cultures.

A number of structural features differentiate these two types of cultures. Household arrangement is one. Nuclear family cultures tend to prefer nuclear households in which the mother, father, and children live under one roof, other kinsmen excluded. Extended family cultures prefer other household arrangements. Nuclear households were preferred by Orchard Town, Juxtlahuaca, and Tarong with 96, 86, and 79 percent of the sample families, respectively, living in such a household. Although some of the families in Taira, Nyansongo, and Khalapur lived in nuclear households, the percentages of 46, 33, and 37, respectively, in no case represented a majority of the sample. The nuclear family cultures tended to have flexible rules governing where a newly married couple should reside in relation to their natal home. The extended family cultures have prescriptive rules of residence; the second generation couple must reside in the household, courtyard, or homestead of either the wife's (uxorilocal) or the husband's (virilocal) parents.

Orchard Town is an example of a culture with a strong preference for neolocal residence. "The husband, wife and their children generally live in a separate dwelling unit. Widowed parents of the husband or wife are possible additions to the household, although such additions are regarded with distaste by most people." However, the mothers of five of the children and the father of one child in the sample were born and brought up in Orchard Town; in three cases both parents were from Orchard Town; both parents were born elsewhere in the remaining fifteen (Fischer and Fischer, 1963, pp. 887–888).

Tarong exemplifies a residence pattern in which if possible both

near homestead of husband's parents

husband and wife live near their natal homes. Although a preference for virilocal residence is born out by the fact that all the married men in Sitio East, the largest hamlet in the community, were born in Tarong, so also were one-third of the married women, and all but one of the remainder were born in adjacent barrios within easy walking distance of their present houses. (Nydegger and Nydegger, 1963, p. 376).

Residence patterns in Juxtlahuaca were similar to those in Tarong. "The ideally stated preference for patrilocal (virilocal) residence is not born out by an actual statistical count. The relationship between adjacent families in the barrio as a whole is as frequently linked through females as through males. This judgment assumes that the criterion of interaction and adjacency is more important than sharing a single common patio area. If the more stringent criterion of sharing common patio is involved, then the ideally stated pattern of patrilocal residence has an edge of about two to one." (Romney and Romney, 1963, p. 589.)

Thus, in the three nuclear family cultures the family might establish a household near either set of grandparents, near both sets of grandparents, or near neither set. No rigid rules governed their choice and the extended family as a corporate land holding unit did not exist. For the three cultures with an extended family organization there were prescriptive rules of virilocal residence.

A sharp distinction was made in Taira between the oldest and younger sons. "There are two types of household in Taira: those of oldest sons, who live in the house of their parents, and those of the younger sons, who establish a nuclear household of their own, which may be near the house of their father. Many young sons, however, leave the central village and settle in its outlying districts or move to the southern part of the island. . . . For a woman it is customary to move to her husband's home if he is an older son or into a house in his village if he is a younger son. In the old days, this usually involved simply a move in the village, since the preference was to marry a woman from the same community. Nowadays there is no clear-cut preference; a woman from central Taira may become the bride of a man from that part of the village, from one of the outlying parts of Taira, or from another village, usually to the north. Of a sample of 55 marriages, 26 of the wives were from Taira, 29 from other villages, 5 of which were immediately adjacent." (Maretzki and Maretzki, 1963, p. 415.) Except for the strict rules governing oldest sons, the residence pattern was not too dissimilar from that of Tarong and Juxtlahuaca, although somewhat stronger bias toward virilocality was manifest.

Residence patterns in Khalapur and Nyansongo were prescriptively virilocal. These rules were required to maintain a patrilineal clan community, which was a basic economic, political, and social unit in these two cultures. The clan community consisted of a group of men all descended through the male line from a real or putative common ancestor. Rules of exogamy required that wives must come from another community with a different descent line, and for the same reason daughters of the community had to emigrate upon marriage. In such residential arrangements a father lived in familiar territory surrounded by his brothers and other patrilineally related male kinsmen, while the mother was a stranger in a strange land. A description of part of the wedding ceremony illustrates the degree of alienation of an inmarrying female in Khalapur. "When a new bride enters her husband's home, she is put 'on display' every afternoon for several days. All the women of the family's lineage are invited to see

A young Khalapur mother with her in-laws

her and her dowry. The bride, her sari pulled over her head and face, sits huddled on the courtyard floor. One by one the visiting women lift her veil and peer at her face, while the bride, with lowered eye-lids, struggles to turn away. . . . No one speaks to the bride, and it would be shameless for her to join in the conversation. . . . The children, both those of the family and those who have come with their mothers, watch the proceedings, and occasionally a little girl, with a troubled expression on her young face, stands thoughtfully viewing the silent figure huddled in the midst of the chattering women." (Minturn and Hitchcock, 1963, p. 256.)

An equally harrowing circumstance is experienced by the Nyansongo bride on her wedding night. Since it is of great importance to the groom to be sexually successful, a number of his young clansmen may attend the nuptial bed—so that if he has difficulty they may "intervene, reprimand the bride, and hold her in position so that penetration can be achieved on the first night" (LeVine and LeVine, 1963, p. 66).

Learning Environments

The corporate patrilineal extended family with its associated prescriptive virilocal rules of residence determines the role of the husband and has important consequences for his relation to his wife and children. Since his parents live in the same house or in the same courtyard, his loyalties are divided between them and his own wife and children. He is dependent upon his father, who, as a senior member of the extended family, has control over its dwellings and land. His mother, who has brought him up, continues to exercise authority over him in domestic matters. Furthermore, since his mother began her life in the community as an outsider she does not easily relinquish the authority that she has finally achieved through her children. His wife is trying to establish herself through her children. The husband is thus torn between the conflicting demands of mother and wife. It is small wonder that he spends less time with his family than where such a conflict does not exist.*

In Juxtlahuaca, Tarong, and Orchard Town a man slept in the same bedroom and usually in the same bed as his wife. It was also customary for the whole family to eat at the same time and place. In contrast, family sleeping and eating patterns were quite different in the three cultures with extended families, particularly Khalapur and Nyansongo.

In Khalapur a man generally slept in the men's quarters which he shared with his brothers and other adult male relatives. This was built near the cattle corral so he could guard his livestock against theft and predation. It was here too that he spent most of his leisure time chatting and gossiping with other men. Although the men sometimes ate in the women's houses, this was not a family affair. "Eating is a strictly private matter in the village. Each man eats either at his own hearth or men's quarters. Each woman takes her food into her own room or into a corner where she can turn her back toward the other women. Children are fed when they demand food and may eat together or separately." (Minturn and Hitchcock, 1963, p. 244.)

The dual household arrangement effectively separates the men from the women and young children and prevents an intimate relationship between the two groups.

Dual households were also preferred in Nyansongo. When they are

---

*Unpublished field notes collected by Susan Abbott on a patrilocal extended family Kikuyu community and by Fatima Mernissa on a patrilocal extended family culture in Morocco support this interpretation.

first married and the children are young, a husband and wife might sleep in the same dwelling, although not ordinarily in the same bed. As soon as the oldest son became pre-adolescent, however, a hut was built near his parents' home and he had to move out of the house to sleep there. When this occurred, the father also usually preferred to sleep there rather than in the house with his wife and young children. This was particularly true if, as often happened in Nyansongo, he had taken a second wife. He preferred to sleep in the boy's house than to risk the jealousy that might result if he close to sleep with his favorite wife. It was also the case that if a man took a job elsewhere he usually would not take his wife and family with him, but would live apart, visiting them only occasionally. If his work was at some distance from Nyansongo, these visits might be a month or more apart and often of only a few days' duration.

In monogamous families in Nyansongo a man would usually eat with his wife and children, but in polygynous families "every wife has to bring the husband a basket of porridge at least once a day, and although he cannot consume all that is brought, he eats at least a mouthful from the basket brought by each wife. The rest of the food is then taken back to be eaten by the children." (LeVine and LeVine, 1963, p. 39.)

It is apparent that in Nyansongo a man was prevented from enjoying an intimate relationship with his wife and children not only by the possibility of friction between his wife and his mother but also, if he was a polygynist, by potential jealousy between his wives.

Family life in Taira resembled that in the three nuclear family cultures in that husband and wife ate together. In the extended family households, however, a grandmother, grandfather, or both would be present at the family meal. Although husbands and wives slept in the same room, ^this was again shared with grandparents in the case of extended households. "Father and mother do not always sleep together, and, even if they do, an infant may sleep between them. When there are several children, another child may sleep next to the father so that in one row there may be mother, a baby, father and an older child. One or two children usually sleep with the grandmother in another corner." (Maretzki and Maretzki, 1963, p. 385.)

In the nuclear family cultures a man had daily opportunity to exchange news with his family at mealtime and intimacies with his wife at night. These exchanges took place much less frequently in Nyansongo and Khalapur and, although it was not reported, the presence of his mother at the table and in the bedroom must have inhibited the free exchange of intimacies between an oldest son and his wife in Taira. The social distance between husband and wife in Khalapur was perhaps the most extreme; a young man who grew up in a similar extended family household in northern India told the authors that he never remembered hearing his mother and father talk to each other.

Another index of the degree of intimacy between husband and wife is whether the husband or any man is permitted to be present at childbirth. In Tarong and in Juxtlahuaca the husband was in the room with the wife, on hand to help if needed. The Nydeggers state the "the husband's presence is essential" (1963, p. 805), and in childbirth they witnessed the husband holding his wife's arm during labor. Tarong midwives were men. Similarly, in Orchard Town in the hospital where women deliver, although it was not reported in the monograph, the probability is that most of the doctors were men. Taira, where there is an equal split in the type of households, was similar to the nuclear household societies in that "the husband may be present during the wife's first delivery, but at subsequent births will wait with some women in the front room" (Maretzki and Maretzki, 1963, p. 457). There was no midwife in Taira at the time of the field work and a medical practitioner, a former World War II corpsman, was called in at childbirth. In Nyansongo and Khalapur it would be inconceivable for a man to be present.

As might be expected, overt aggression between husband and wife was most common in the cultures with extended families. In the ethnographic descriptions no wife-beating in Orchard Town was mentioned. In Tarong and Juxtlahuaca wife-beating was mentioned only as a punishment for adultery (Nydegger and Nydegger, 1963, p. 760; Romney and Romney, 1963, p. 610), and no incident was reported during the field work even though one husband in Juxtlahuaca was aware that his wife was sleeping with another man. In Taira the Maretzkis mentioned disputes between husbands and wives some of which were settled by the husband's hitting the wife (Maretzki and Maretzki, 1963, p. 421). In Khalapur "a man, if angry may beat his wife . . ." (Minturn and Hitchcock, 1963, p. 240.) Similarly, in Nyansongo a husband had a recognized right to beat his wife if she was disobedient (LeVine and LeVine, 1963, p. 43).

The intimacy of the household also has the effect of decreasing the social distance between a man and his children. Our data indicate that children who grew up in the three nuclear family cultures interacted with their fathers more frequently than children in the three extended family cultures. Less than 1 percent of the social acts of the children of non-nuclear societies—Taira, Nyansongo and Khalapur— were directed toward their fathers (.001, .002, and .003, respectively). For the other three nuclear cultures the proportions were Orchard Town and Juxtlahuaca, .01; Tarong, .02. As can be inferred

Fathers and sons in rice paddy, Tarong

Fathers + sons
do interact
(see p. 123) ←

Fathers and sons, Juxtlahuaca

Father and son in Orchard Town

(see p. 123)

from the low proportion scores, many of the sample children were not observed to interact with their fathers at all. This was particularly true in Taira, Khalapur, and Nyansongo. On the other hand, over half of the Tarongan children were observed interacting with their fathers, and approximately one-third of the children of Orchard Town and Juxtlahuaca were seen to do so.

Since few of the observations were made in the evenings, which in all cultures is the time that the father was most likely to interact with his family, these scores underrepresent his parental role. There is no reason to suspect, however, that a more adequate sample of the behavior of fathers would change the ordering of the six cultures with respect to the degree of father-child interactions.

Summary

Orchard Town, Juxtlahuaca, and Tarong, the three cultures whose children had positive scores on Dimension B, that is, were higher on acts sociably, assaults sociably, and touches, than they were on assaults and reprimands, had the following characteristics: their domestic arrangements were based on the independent nuclear family and the nuclear household in which the father ate at the same table with his wife and children, slept with his wife, was present when she delivered her babies, and was reported to have helped her care for infants. He was unlikely to express his anger to his wife by physical assault, and, although he did not spend a great deal of time with his children, they tended to direct their behavior toward him when he was present.

Taira, Khalapur, and Nyansongo, whose children were higher on assaults and reprimands than on acts sociably, assaults sociably, and touches had contrasting domestic arrangements: the patrilineal extended family, a corporate property-owning group maintained by

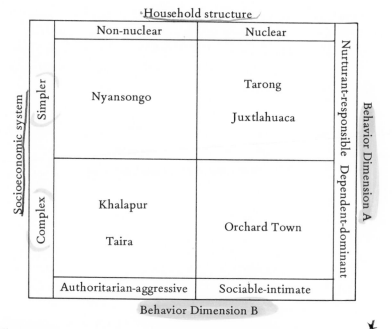

Figure 14. A paradigm arranging the six cultures by culture type and two dimensions of social behavior.

prescriptive virilocal residence, and authority vested in a member of the grandparents' generation were the focus of domestic life.

CONCLUSION

Two independent cultural features—the complexity of the socio-economic system, and the composition of the household—were shown to be predictive of the social behavior of children. Children brought up in complex cultures tended to be more dependent-dominant and less nurturant-responsible than children brought up in simpler cultures; and children brought up in cultures where the composition of the household was ideally nuclear were more sociable-intimate and less authoritarian-aggressive than children brought up in cultures where the ideal composition of the household was not nuclear. The relation between these variables is shown paradigmatically in Figure 14.

5   Differences within Cultures

Variations in the socioeconomic system and the household structure at the cultural level have been shown to influence the learning environments of children, causing their social behavior to be predictably different. In making this analysis we classified each culture on a normative basis. Cultures were either simple or complex, expected their children to help with domestic chores or go to school, favored nuclear or some other form of household. For many of these variables, despite preferences dictated by the culture, there was variation within each community among the families of our sample. In our original plan we had hoped to discover whether such differences had the same effect as they did across cultures.

Certain constraints, however, make the inquiry into the effects of differences in learning environments difficult. In the first place, we did not anticipate many of the features that we discovered largely on a post hoc basis to be important as determinants of the social behavior of children at the cultural level. Consequently, variables such as the mother's workload and the involvement of the father in

130

domestic affairs were not measured for each household. In the second place, the effect of other features cannot be tested because no within-culture variation occurs. A given degree of socioeconomic complexity is a variable that characterizes all the children of a given culture. Finally, some of the features for which we have evidence vary within all or some of the cultures but, as will be discussed later, in such a biased manner that their effect cannot be appropriately tested.

We had hoped that the number and type of economic tasks and chores assigned to children might be a variable whose effect could be measured within as well as across cultures. However, many chores were sex-typed and performed only by older children. With this constraint it turned out that many chores were performed either by all or by none of the children in a given group. Furthermore, our measures were not refined enough to assess the relative responsibility required by different tasks or the amount of time sample children spent performing each. Therefore, a within-culture test of the effect of economic tasks could not be made.

Whether or not children were customarily assigned the task of caring for infants was shown to be related, at the cultural level, to relatively high positive scores on Dimension A. The children of cultures that customarily expected their children to take care of younger brothers and sisters tended to be more nurturant and responsible and less dependent and dominant than cultures where the assignment of such a task was not customary. There was enough variation in our measures of child care to make within-culture comparison possible. To test the effect of differences we used scores controlled for sex and age.

Several individual scores of child care were available to test the hypothesis. One was based on the mother's answer to the question,

A)

"What chores do you expect P to do?" The association between her mentioning child care as a chore expected of P and P's score on Dimension A is shown in Table 23, Test A. The test was made separately for each sex-age group. Since the number of cases is so small for each group, significance tests are not appropriate and only the direction of association has been reported. As can be seen, no test can be made for ten of the twenty-four groups. Since caring for younger siblings was not considered appropriate for children in our

Table 23. Direction of association between Dimension A (nurturant-responsible versus dependent-dominant) and three tests estimating child care as a task.

Sex	Age	Test[a]	Taira	Tarong	Khala-pur	Juxtla-huaca	Orchard Town	Nyan-songo
Boys	3–6	A	+	+	0	0	0	+
		B	+	+	+	+	+	+
		C	–	0	+	–	–	–
	7–11	A	–	+	+	–	0	0
		B	+	+	+	+	0	–
		C	0	+	+	+	+	0
Girls	3–6	A	+	+	0	0	0	+
		B	+	+	+	–	+	+
		C	0	+	+	0	+	+
	7–11	A	+	0	+	+	0	+
		B	+	+	+	–	+	+
		C	–	–	–	+	+	+

[a] A: mother's report that this was assigned as a task. B: Proportion of interaction with infant targets over all targets. C: Older and middle versus younger and only positions in the sibling order. 0 indicates that no test could be made; + indicates a positive association; – indicates a negative association.

132

age range in Orchard Town, no mother mentioned it as a chore. The fact that it was not mentioned for young children in Khalapur and Juxlahuaca and for older boys in Nyansongo may also reflect cultural values rather than actual practice. The fact that in the last two groups children were observed in the baby-tending role supports this interpretation. Whether a mother's report is taken as a measure of her attitude or a report of actual behavior, there is reasonably strong support for its positive association with Dimension A. In eight of the ten age groups a child whose mother reported requiring child care was on the average more nurturant-responsible and less dominant-dependent than a child in the same sex-age group whose mother made no such claim. If the sex-age groups are pooled across cultures the association is positive and statistically significant ($P < .01$).

A second question from the mother interviews was used in Chapter 4 to estimate the cultural attitude toward trusting children to care for infants. When asked "Who took care of _____ when he was a baby?" some mothers named an older sibling as caretaker. If this statement reflects a mother's attitude and policy, it may be assumed that all her children will have been required to take care of their younger siblings. This indirect measure of task assignment could be used as a test of the hypothesis in only six of the twenty-four sex-age groups and showed no relation to Dimension A.

It has been suggested that the frequency with which a child interacts with infants compared to his interaction with older children and adults may influence his or her score on Dimension A. This assumption will be discussed in more detail in Chapter 7. The association between the proportion of a child's acts directed toward infant targets and his or her score on Dimension A is presented in Table 23, Test B. As can be seen, a test could be made for each group except older boys in Orchard Town, none of whom were ever observed interacting with an infant. This test also showed general support for the hypothesis. Twenty of twenty-three tests were in the positive direction, and for pooled sex-age groups the results were statistically significant (P < .001).

A final test of the effect of caring for children on Dimension A is provided by a child's position in the sibling order. The Kikuyu of Kenya have an adage, "The youngest child is a spoiled child." They explain this by saying that, since they have no younger siblings to take care of, they have no way of learning not to be selfish. Although some sample children were assigned the task of caring for younger courtyard cousins, in the majority of cases if a child was assigned a baby-sitting task, his or her charge was a younger sibling. Test C shows the difference on Dimension A between children who had younger siblings (older and middle in the sibling order) and those who did not (youngest and only). Although the association tended to be negative for the younger boys and split for older girls, it was positive for each of the other two sex-age groups where a test could be made. The association between the pooled score and Dimension A was positive and statistically significant (P < .001).

The variables assumed to be related to Dimension B at the cultural level were the participation of a child's father in domestic affairs and a child's membership in a nuclear household. Children brought up in cultures favoring nuclear households, in which the father ate and slept with the mother and helped her with child care, were more sociable and less aggressive than children brought up in non-nuclear households.

Within-culture tests of the effect of whether or not a child was living in a nuclear household at the time of the study turned out to be difficult, their results ambiguous. When the sample was broken

134

down into sex-age groups, an appropriate test could be made on only six of the twenty-four groups. In the others there was either no contrast whatsover in household type, or else only one child represented a deviation from the cultural norm. Of the six cases where a test could be made there was a positive association (by a χ^2 test) for young boys in Taira, older boys in Tarong and Khalapur, young girls in Khalapur, and older girls in Tarong. The association was negative for the older girls of Taira, and there was no relation for the older boys in this culture. If the above tests were pooled for each culture the association reached an acceptable level of statistical significance ($P < .05$) for both Tarong and Khalapur but not for Taira.

The other two measures that were assumed to be related to Dimension B at the cultural level—the amount of interactions of a child with his or her father and the report on the mother interviews that the father helped care for P as a baby—were so biased in their distribution over sex-age groups that no appropriate test of their effects within cultures could be made.

In sum, then, the question of the correspondence of the effect of variables within and across cultures remains unanswered. Such evidence as there is suggests that they have a comparable effect. Shweder (1973), using some of the same data, takes the opposite position. He shows that the correlation matrix that we used to construct Dimension A is not similar to matrices based on children's scores within each culture. Shweder draws this conclusion on the basis of only six of the twelve behaviors. Longabaugh (1966), using all twelve behaviors and factor analysis, draws the opposite conclusion. We suspect that some variables have identical effects within and across cultures, while others may be quite different. The answer to this important question will have to await testing by better measures on larger samples.

6   Sex and Age

The dimension scores used in the preceding two chapters were
designed to maximize cultural differences and discount difference
due to sex and age. This was done by averaging the scores of boys and
girls in each age group to obtain an aggregate score for each culture.
For the present inquiry a procedure is required that will discount
cultural differences and highlight differences due to sex and age. To
accomplish this, scores were standardized by culture, a procedure
resulting in twelve sets with the same means (zero) and the same
standard deviation (one) for each culture. Thus it was possible to
calculate a pooled score for the effects of sex and age with the direct
effects of culture ruled out.

Means were then calculated for the pooled standardized scores of
boys and girls in three age groups: 3–5, 6–7, and 8–11. These groupings were chosen so that any marked shift in the rate of change
represented in the sample might be reflected, and, at the same time, a
reasonable sample size maintained for each point. In the 3–5 age
group there were twenty-five girls and twenty-four boys; for the 6–7

But now

age group there were fifteen girls and twenty-two boys; and for the 8–11 age group there were twenty-seven girls and twenty-one boys.

The means for each of the twelve types of behavior were then plotted for each sex-age group and arranged according to similarity of pattern (see Figure 15). The top rows contain behaviors that decrease or remain constant with age while the bottom rows contain those that increase or remain constant with age. In the left-hand column are behaviors in which scores for girls are higher than those for boys. In the middle column girls score less than boys, and in the right-hand column the scores are similar for the two groups.

To reduce the redundancy in the data the twelve behaviors were combined into six clusters on the basis of two criteria: if two behaviors showed similar sex differences and/or similar changes with age they were combined. Thus, *touches* and *seeks help,* which are both more frequent proportionally in the behavior of young girls and which both decrease with age, were combined into cluster 1 and labeled *intimate-dependent. Offers help* and *offers support* are also more frequent proportionally for girls and increased for girls with age; they were combined to form cluster 2, *nurturant.* Boys scored higher on *assaults, insults,* and *horseplay,* and these combined categories form cluster 3, *aggressive.* Similarly, *seeks dominance* and *seeks attention,* also more frequent in boys, were combined to form cluster 4, *dominant-dependent.* There were no sex differences in *acts sociably,* and the decrease with age was similar for boys and girls. Since no other behavior was similar by the two criteria, this behavior alone makes up cluster 5, *sociable.* Cluster 6, *Pro-social,* combines *suggests responsibly* and *reprimands,* both of which increase with age and show no significant sex differences.

The next step was to create six new scores based on the above

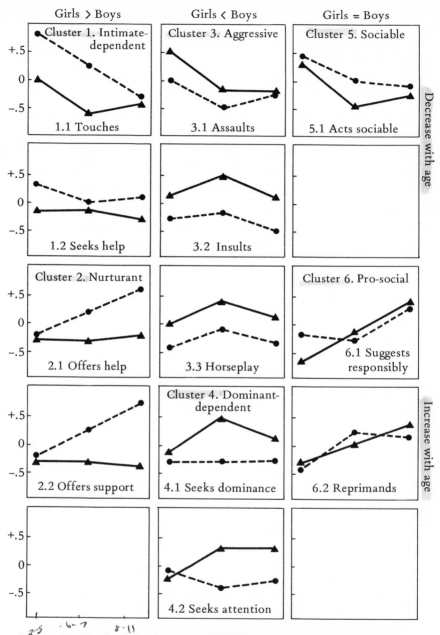

Figure 15. Twelve behavior types plotted by sex and age and arranged by similarity of pattern (girls ●; boys ▲).

analysis by summing the scores of the individual behaviors in each cluster and calculating the means for each cluster for both boys and girls in the 3–5 age group, the 6–7 age group, and the 8–11 age group. These means are plotted on Figure 16 (p. 143), arranged in the same way as Figure 15. The combination of rows and columns thus represents a contrast between behavior which decreases with age and might be considered childish (see top row) with more adult behavior (bottom row), and contrasts behaviors observed more frequently in girls (column 1) with those found more frequently in boys (column 2) and those where there were no sex differences (column 3).

AGE BY SEX DIFFERENCES

To estimate the differential effect of age on the sexes, a correlation (Pearson r) was calculated between age and each behavioral cluster for both boys and girls. The changes with age are shown in Tables 24, 25, and 26. It can be seen that on the intimate-dependent cluster girls decrease significantly (r = .36; P < .001) and the decrease is steady, while boys show no significant change. Conversely, for the nurturant cluster girls increase steadily and significantly (r = .51; P < .001) and, again, boys do not change. It is unlikely that such striking results for girls could have been obtained unless the effect was general across all six cultures, and Table 24 indicates that such is the case. With the exception of Orchard Town the changes are in the expected direction and half the correlations at +.50 or greater. For boys, with a few exceptions, the correlations are low and inconsistent. There are two significant decreases in the nurturant behavior of boys: one in Tarong (r = −.82; P < .001), the other in Orchard Town (r = −.79; P < .001). In both cases the change is a regression toward the cross-cultural mean—Orchard Town young boys ranking

139

Table 24. Correlations (Pearson *r*) between the ages of the children and their scores on the indicated behavior clusters.

Culture	Intimate-dependent (seeks help and touches)		Nurturant (gives help and gives support)	
	Girls	Boys	Girls	Boys
All cultures[a]	−.36***[b]	−.14	.51***	−.02
Nyansongo	−.50	.39	.29	−.84**
Juxtlahuaca	−.31	.05	.43	−.07
Tarong	−.51*	−.82***	.62*	.19
Taira	−.40	.24	.41	.57*
Khalapur	−.74	.29	.61*	−.35
Orchard Town	.04	−.79***	.66**	.10

[a]Scores for "All cultures" are standardized for each culture and pooled.
[b]Significance levels are indicated as follows: $P < .05^*, < .01^{**}, < .001^{***}$.

first among the boys of the six cultures in *seeking help,* Tarongan young boys in *touching.* A similar interpretation can be made for the decrease in nurturant behavior in Nyansongo (r = −.84; P < .01), whose younger boys scored significantly higher on *offers help* than any of the other boys in the six cultures. Tairan young boys, who increase significantly in nurturant behavior (r = .57; P < .05), again suggesting a regression toward the mean, rank fifth in *offering support* and sixth in *offering help.*

Figure 16 suggests a slight increase with age for both sexes on the dominant-dependent cluster and a slight decrease with age for the aggressive cluster. Table 25 indicates, however, that these trends are weak and do not approach an acceptable level of significance. The age trends for individual cultures on these clusters are quite inconsis-

Table 25. Correlations (Pearson r) between the ages of the children and their scores on the indicated behavior clusters.

Culture	Dominant-dependent (seeks dominance, seeks attention)		Aggressive (insults, assaults, horseplay)	
	Girls	Boys	Girls	Boys
All cultures[a]	.05	.09	−.02	−.13
Nyansongo	−.32	.10	−.16	−.16
Juxtlahuaca	.42	.49	.05	.11
Tarong	−.15	.24	.03	.43
Taira	.12	.04	−.06	−.38
Khalapur	.32	−.02	−.15	−.51*[b]
Orchard Town	.28	.14	.05	.21

[a]Scores for "All cultures" are standardized for each culture and pooled.
[b]Significance values are indicated as follows: $P < .05$*.

tent. In sum, analysis suggests that there is little change for either boys or girls during the 3–11 age period on either the dominant-dependent or aggressive clusters.

The third column of Figure 16 contains two clusters in which changes with age are similar for boys and girls. As indicated in Table 26, their scores decrease on the sociable cluster—for boys $r = -.17$, for girls $r = -.27$ ($P < .01$). Both boys and girls increase on their pro-social behavior as they get older, with scores of $r = +.47$ ($P < .01$) and $+.33$ ($P < .01$), respectively.

When each culture is tested separately, the girls are again more consistent than the boys. In all six cultures their scores decrease for the sociable cluster and increase for the pro-social cluster. For the boys

Table 26. Correlations (Pearson r) between the ages of the children and their scores on the indicated behavior clusters.

Culture	Sociable (acts sociably)		Pro-social (suggests responsibly, reprimands)	
	Girls	Boys	Girls	Boys
All cultures[a]	−.27**[b]	−.17	.33**	.47**
Nyansongo	−.16	.28	.66	.79**
Juxtlahuaca	−.48	−.77**	.56	.42
Tarong	−.35	−.54	.20	.68**
Taira	−.29	.28	.20	−.02
Khalapur	−.06	−.21	.19	.65**
Orchard Town	−.42	−.01	.48	.35

[a]Scores for "All cultures" are standardized for each culture and pooled.
[b]Significance values are indicated as follows: $P < .05^*, < .01^{**}$.

there are three exceptions: Nyansongo and Orchard Town boys increase on sociable behavior as they get older, and Tairan boys show a slight reversal on the pro-social cluster.

DISCUSSION

Because most research on changes in children's behavior with age has been concerned with their cognitive abilities rather than with their social behavior, it is difficult to compare our results with previous findings. The so-called 5–7 shift in children's mode of thinking that has been repeatedly demonstrated (White, 1968; Super, 1970) in both Western and non-Western societies does not seem to apply generally to the social behavior of children. Age effects on the six cluster scores for both boys and girls show either no change or a monotonic change

during the 3–11 period. This, however, is partly an artifact of combining behavior types, as we have, into clusters. There are some indi-
cations of a 5–7 shift for some of the individual behavior types. As
shown in Figure 15 boys' scores go down steeply between the 3–5
and 6–7 age periods and level off between 6–7 and 8–11 for *touches,
assaults,* and *acts sociably.* Their scores peak at 6–7 for *insults, seeks*

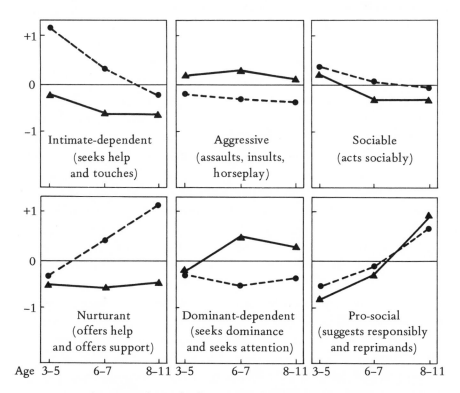

Figure 16. Changes with age for boys (▲) and girls (●) for six behavior clusters
(scores standardized by culture and pooled). p. 139 (top)

dominance, and *horseplay.* Age changes for girls are more monotonic; their only marked inflection is for *assaults.*

Cross-cultural evidence (Whiting and Child, 1953) indicates that socializing agents in all cultures exert pressure on children, once the infancy period has been passed, to be less dependent and less aggressive. Evidence from the mother interviews suggests that this is true in the six cultures as well. If such pressure is successful we would expect a decreasing trend with age for these two types of behavior. Our data show a decrease—an expected one—in intimate-dependent behavior, especially for girls, but not for the dominant-dependent cluster. *Seeks dominance,* one of its components, in fact increases with age for the boys. The aggressive cluster also remains constant for both sexes over the 3–11 age period. *Assaults,* one of the components of this cluster, does decrease, especially for boys. The decrease, however, is neutralized by a slight increase in *horseplay.* The decrease in age for *sociable* behavior perhaps can be attributed to socialization pressure since sociability is correlated with dependency (Edwards, 1972).

The increase with age for the nurturant and pro-social clusters is accompanied by an increase in the assignment of economic and child care responsibilities (see Chapter 4). These findings correspond in general to the cross-cultural findings of Barry, Bacon, and Child (1957). Based on reports of 110 societies, their study indicates that across their sample pressure was exerted on children to be nurturant and responsible. If pro-social behavior reflects responsibility, then both these types of behavior in our sample should increase with age, as predicted.

The Bacon, Barry, and Child finding that pressures on these behavior systems are greater for girls than for boys is reflected in our nurturant but not our pro-social cluster. In their sample of societies,

144

self-reliance and achievement are stressed for boys. We have no direct measure of either of these behaviors, but if *seeks dominance* and *seeks attention* are equated with achievement, our findings replicate theirs.

The increase in pro-social behavior between the ages of 3 and 11 is of particular interest as it may be related to the development of what Kohlberg (1969) has labeled conventional moral reasoning. Evidence from this study indicates that between these years children were being taught the rules of proper behavior. During this time, 90 percent of the instigations they received from their mothers were either orders to perform tasks or suggestions as to proper behavior. Children imitated these patterns in interacting with peers, instructing them in the rules of behavior which they themselves were in the process of learning. Detailed analysis of the content of these pro-social demands at various ages might furnish detailed descriptions of the transition from pragmatic moral reasoning based on fear of punishment to reasoning in terms of conventions.

SEX AND AGE DIFFERENCES

The changes by age for boys and girls reported above do not take into account the differences between boys and girls at different ages. Sex differences by age can be seen by inspection of Figure 16. Our analysis here is not concerned with children at the three age periods shown in this figure but is restricted to the two age periods for which the sample was matched: 3–6 and 7–11.

Differences between the scores for boys and for girls on the intimate-dependent and nurturant clusters at both the younger and older ages are shown in Table 27. The comparison is made for each culture and summarized for all cultures. Girls score higher than boys

Table 27. Mean differences between boys and girls aged 3–6 and 7–11, for all and for each culture on the intimate-dependent and nurturant clusters.

Culture	Intimate-dependent (touches, seeks help)		Nurturant (offers help, offers support)	
	3–6	7–11	3–6	7–11
All cultures[a]	1.2**[b]	0.4	1.2	1.7***
Nyansongo	1.8	−0.1	−1.3	2.1*
Juxtlahuaca	1.8**	0.2	0.7	2.4*
Tarong	0.4	0.8	1.2*	2.3*
Taira	1.7*	0.9	1.4*	0.2
Khalapur	2.3	−1.2*	−0.7	1.8
Orchard Town	−0.7	1.6	−0.5	1.6

[a]Scores for "All cultures" are standardized for each culture and pooled.
[b]+ indicates girls > boys; – indicates boys > girls. Significance of differences estimated by t tests is indicated as follows: $P < .05^*$, $< .01^{**}$, $< .001^{***}$.

on the intimate-dependent cluster at the younger age period, but this difference disappears in the older group. The converse is true for the nurturant cluster. There is no significant or consistent sex difference at the 3–6 age period, but girls are markedly more nurturant than boys in the 7–11 sample.

Scores for boys are for the most part higher than those for girls on both the dominant-dependent and aggressive clusters (see Table 28). For the former, although at the younger age period the difference on the pooled scores is not statistically significant, boys score higher than girls in five of the six cultures, significantly so in Khalapur. At the older age period, the difference for the pooled scores is significant ($P < .01$). The differences for all six cultures are in the predicted direction, and significant for Nyansongo.

The aggressive cluster in Table 28 is clearly sex-typed; with one

Table 28. Mean differences between boys and girls aged 3–6 and 7–11, for all and for each culture on the dominant-dependent and aggressive clusters.

Culture	Dominant-dependent (seeks dominance, seeks attention)		Aggressive (assaults, insults, horseplay)	
	3–6	7–11	3–6	7–11
All cultures[a]	−0.57[b]	−0.94**	−1.51*	−1.37**
Nyansongo	−0.61	−1.43*	−0.23	0.26
Juxtlahuaca	−0.65	−1.23	−1.69	−2.06
Tarong	−0.67	−1.56	−1.72*	−2.35*
Taira	−0.29	−0.51	−2.48	−1.28
Khalapur	−1.42*	−0.08	−2.19	−0.50
Orchard Town	0.21	−1.03	−0.19	−1.53

[a]The scores for "All cultures" are standardized for each culture and pooled.
[b]+ indicates girls > boys, – indicates boys > girls. Significance of differences estimated by t tests are as follows: $P < .05*, < .01**, < .001***$.

exception boys score higher than girls in all cultures at both age periods and the difference for the pooled samples are significant. Nyansongo is the only aberrant culture; there is little difference in either age group and the girls score higher in the 7–11 period.

Sociable and pro-social behavior are not sex-typed. Although there is a slight tendency for girls to be more sociable, it only reaches significance in older Khalapur girls. Pro-social behavior is more frequent among the 3–6-year-old girls, but by 7–11 the trend has reversed. It seems clear that this behavior is determined by age rather than by sex. If one's score on this behavior is taken as a measure of maturity it may reflect the fact the girls develop more rapidly than boys (see Table 29).

In sum, girls are more intimate-dependent than boys, but the

Table 29. Mean differences between boys and girls aged 3–6 and 7–11, for all and for each culture on the sociable and pro-social clusters.

Culture	Sociable (acts sociably)		Pro-social (suggests responsibly, reprimands)	
	3–6	7–11	3–6	7–11
All cultures[a]	0.2[b]	0.3	0.4	−0.2
Nyansongo	0.0	0.1	0.7	−1.3
Juxtlahuaca	−0.9	−0.7	0.1	0.6
Tarong	−0.4	0.3	1.3	−0.3
Taira	0.7	0.8	0.2	0.1
Khalapur	0.8	1.2*	0.7	−1.3
Orchard Town	0.7	−0.2	−0.5	0.8

[a]The scores for "All cultures" are standardized for each culture and pooled.
[b]+ indicates girls > boys, −indicates boys > girls. Signifiance of differences estimated by t tests are as follows: $P < .05$*.

differences are significant only in the 3–6 age group; girls are also more nurturant, significantly so at 7–11. Boys tend to be more dominant-dependent and are significantly more aggressive. These findings are remarkably consistent in all six societies.

DISCUSSION

The reason for the consistency of the above sex differences across cultures is an open question. It is possible that girls' higher scores at 3–6 years on *seeks help* and *touches* reflect less severe socialization pressure to give up these habits, and that the boys' higher scores at this age on *seeks dominance* and *aggression* reflect either less socialization pressure against these behaviors than that experienced by girls or more encouragement, perhaps motivated by transcultural stereo-types of masculine behavior. On the other hand, the difference may be the result of innate sex-linked characteristics.

One of the authors (Whiting and Edwards, 1973) has argued that touching behavior and horseplay are the best candidates for innate characteristics. These behaviors can be described as alternate forms of seeking and offering physical contact and are assumed to be an innate response of young animals and humans.

Seeking help, which is more frequent in girls, and *seeking attention* and *dominance*, which are more frequent in boys, may be alternative styles for getting others to help satisfy egoistic dependent needs. It should be noted that girls decrease significantly in their mode of dependency during the same period that they increase proportionate-ly in nurturant behavior, a behavior which, it will be remembered, is negatively correlated with the egoistic behaviors *seeks help, seeks dominance,* and *seeks attention.*

Differences between boys and girls at the older age levels are more likely to be learned than innately determined. The degree to which such learning is accomplished by direct tuition, by task assignment, or by identification with adult male and female role models is diffi-cult to determine. In all six cultures girls are more commonly assigned the task of caring for infant siblings than are boys. The increase in nurturant behavior occurs during the period when half of the girls between the ages of 5 and 10 (excluding Orchard Town) care for infants. However, although girls take care of infants more fre-quently than boys (P < .05), the difference between the nurturance scores of girls and boys at 6–7 and 8–11 years (see Figure 16) cannot be accounted for by this responsibility alone. Role modeling undoubt-edly also contributes to the discrepancy.

The mother as a role model is more available to the growing girl than to the boy. In all the societies girls were found in the company of their mothers more often than boys were. This finding has been replicated in the studies of the Munroes (1971), Nerlove (1971), and Ember (1973). Girls in the six cultures did significantly more house-cleaning (P < .001) and more food preparation, cooking, and grinding (P < .001), all tasks which kept them indoors or in the immediate vicinity of the house and under the supervision of their mothers. With the exception of house-cleaning these tasks are obviously concerned with the welfare of others and are training in anticipating and meeting the needs of others—behaviors which we have classified as *nurturant*.

Evidence that indoor chores influence children's social behavior is also furnished by Ember's study (1973) in Kenya. Boys who had no sisters of appropriate age and hence had to perform indoor chores more frequently than other boys were observed in all situations to be less dominant-dependent and less aggressive than their peers.

The effect of greater contact with infants and mothers on social behavior will be discussed in the next chapter. Girls interact with infants significantly more frequently than boys (P < .01). They also interact more frequently with their own mothers (P < .05 at 3–6; P < .01 at 7–11). As will be seen, infants draw nurturance, mothers intimate-dependency.

In sum, the learning environment of girls in all of the six societies is different from that of boys. Girls are more frequently in the house and yard with adults and infants, performing chores which require nurturant behavior, responsibility, and obedience. Boys are more frequently (P < .05) in pastures herding animals (Minturn and Lambert,

1964) and thus further from home. They are supervised less by adults and interact more with peers. The difference in the cast of characters with whom they interact may well be one of the important determinants of their proportionately higher score on social aggression.

7 The Status of the Target

It is improbable that the children of our sample behaved the same way toward adults, children, and peers. One has a better chance of getting away with insulting or assaulting a younger sibling than a parent. Help is more likely to be needed by infants than by adults. To what extent does the status of the person with whom a child is interacting—the target of his or her social behavior—have the discriminative power to evoke or inhibit behavior? What types of targets have such power and what types of behavior are so influenced? Is there uniformity across cultures of such target effects?

Anticipating that the status of the person with whom P interacted would be important, the sex, age, and kin relation to P was identified for the object or target of every act. Where no such person could be specified, the act was considered to be individual rather than social and was excluded. In a few instances the target was an animal or a group; these have been dropped from our analysis.

To make all distinctions by sex, age, and kinship was not feasible. Too few children in the sample interacted with people of precisely the same status, as defined by all these characteristics. Certain infrequently occurring categories either had to be dropped or combined with others. The following three categories were finally chosen: parents, peers, and infants. They represented 80 percent of the targets of all observed acts—11, 54, and 15 percent, respectively. Adults other than parents were omitted, since they represented such diverse categories as aunts, uncles, grandfathers, grandmothers, teachers, and other nonrelatives. Adolescents were also omitted because they occurred as targets with low frequency and because their status was ambiguous, being intermediate between older peers and younger adults. Peers could have been distinguished by sex and age, but preliminary analysis indicated that these differences controlled far less of the variance than the differences between parents, peers, and infants. We wanted to distinguish between fathers and mothers but their proportion scores were so low—1 and 10 percent, respectively— that we could not do so.

For each of the three targets the proportion scores for each of the twelve behaviors were standardized by culture. These were then pooled and the mean calculated. The results are plotted in Figure 17. The graphs are arranged to group the behaviors in the same six clusters used for the analysis of sex and age differences. As can be seen, the behaviors of each cluster show a similar pattern in relation to the three targets; therefore, it seemed justified to combine them into clusters as follows: (1) *Nurturant* (*offers help* and *offers support*); (2) *Pro-social* (*suggests responsibly* and *reprimands*); (3) *Aggressive* (*horseplay, insults,* and *assaults*); (4) *Sociable* (*acts sociably*); (5) *Intimate-dependent* (*touches* and *seeks help*) and (6) *Dominant-dependent* (*seeks dominance* and *seeks attention*). As before, each cluster score consisted of simply summing the scores of their compo-

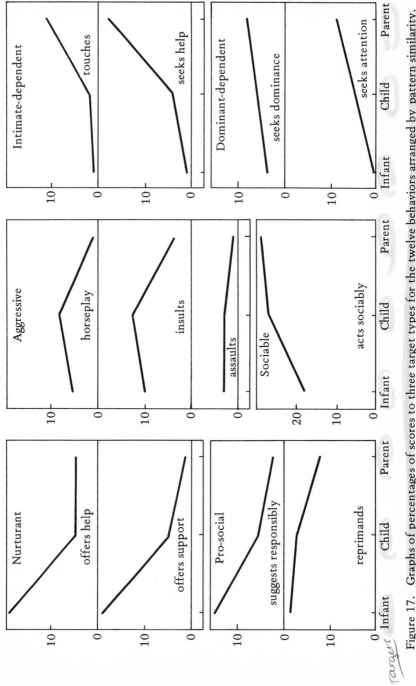

Figure 17. Graphs of percentages of scores to three target types for the twelve behaviors arranged by pattern similarity.

nent behaviors. In this case, however, there were some children in the sample who never reacted to certain target types and had to be dropped from calculations involving that target. When this was done, the sample for each target type was 93 for infants, 105 for parents, and 133 for peers as targets. The means for each of the six behavior clusters that were directed toward the three target types are shown in Figure 18.

This figure indicates that the three target types have strong discriminative power to evoke or inhibit some of the social behavior clusters in children. The power of infants to evoke nurturance and of parents to evoke intimate-dependent and inhibit aggressive behavior is particularly striking. The pro-social, sociable, and dominant-dependent clusters are less strongly focused on one target type. Even small differences, however, are statistically significant: for a 2 percent differents P < .05; for a 3 percent difference P < .01; and for any differences greater than 3 percent the significance level was less than .001. Thus, all the differences are significant with the exception of the proportion of nurturance to peer versus parent and the proportion of prosocial behavior to infant versus peer.

Perhaps a more interesting way of arranging the data of Figure 18 is shown in Table 30. In this table the six behavior clusters are arranged in rank order for each target. The percentages on which the rank order is based are also indicated. The odds are better than 2:1 for a child in our sample interacting with an infant to be either nurturant or aggressive; if the child is interacting with a peer to be either sociable or aggressive; and if the child is interacting with one of his or her parents to be either intimate-dependent or sociable. It is also a good bet that he or she will not be intimate-dependent or dominant-dependent to infants, intimate-dependent or nurturant to a peer or pro-social, or aggressive to a parent.

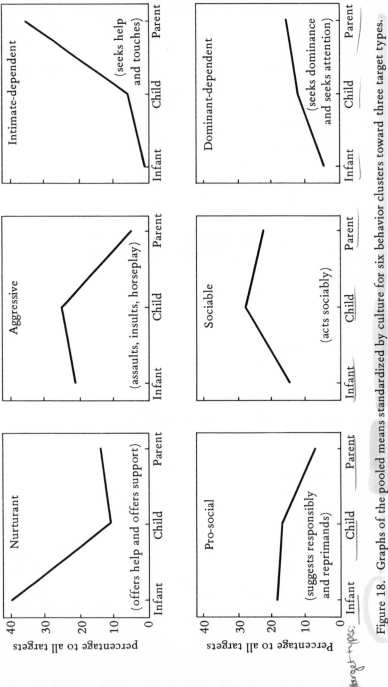

Figure 18. Graphs of the pooled means standardized by culture for six behavior clusters toward three target types. Statistical significance between points can be estimated as follows: < 2 n.g, 2–1.5 ($P < .05$), > 3 ($P < .001$).

Table 30. Percentages of scores on the six behavior clusters to three targets arranged in rank order.

Infants		Peers		Parents	
Nurturant	40	Sociable	28	Intimate-dependent	36
Aggressive	21	Aggressive	24	Sociable	23
Pro-social	18	Pro-social	17	Dominant-dependent	16
Sociable	14	Dominant-dependent	12	Nurturant	12
Dominant-dependent	5	Nurturant	11	Pro-social	8
Intimate-dependent	2	Intimate-dependent	7	Aggressive	5

p. 158

Table 31 compares the rank order of behavior clusters to the three target types for each culture with that for the pooled score. Considerable uniformity in the rank order of these behavior clusters across cultures can be noted. When the rank orders of each culture are intercorrelated (Spearman Rho), the greatest similarity across the six cultures in the discriminative power of targets is for infants. Nurturance is the most common response to infants in all cultures, and intimate-dependent the least common in all but one. The rank order of the clusters for Tarong and Khalapur are identical. This is also the case for Orchard Town and Nyansongo. The greatest divergence is between Taira and Juxtlahuaca, but even for this pair the value of the correlation (Spearman Rho) is +.54. The median value for all pairs is +.83, and only three pairs fall below an acceptable significance level.

Table 31. A comparison between cultures of the rank order of percentages of six behavior clusters to each of three targets.

Target	Behavior cluster	All cultures	Taira	Tarong	Khala-pur	Juxtla-huaca	Orchard Town	Nyan-songo
Infants	Nurturant	1	1	1	1	1	1	1
	Aggressive	2	2	2	2	3	3	3
	Pro-social	3	3	4	4	4	2	2
	Sociable	4	5	3	3	2	4	4
	Dominant-dependent	5	4	5	5	6	5	5
	Intimate-dependent	6	6	6	6	5	6	6

Median Rho between all pairs = +.83

Target	Behavior cluster	All cultures	Taira	Tarong	Khala-pur	Juxtla-huaca	Orchard Town	Nyan-songo
Peers	Sociable	1	2	1	2	1	1	2
	Aggressive	2	1	2	1	3	2	3
	Pro-social	3	3	4	3	4	3	1
	Dominant-dependent	4	4	5	4	5	4	5
	Nurturant	5	5	3	5	2	6	4
	Intimate-dependent	6	6	6	6	6	5	6

Median Rho between all pairs = +.66

Target	Behavior cluster	All cultures	Taira	Tarong	Khala-pur	Juxtla-huaca	Orchard Town	Nyan-songo
Parents	Intimate-dependent	1	4	1	1	1	3	4
	Sociable	2	5	2	4	2	2	1
	Dominant-dependent	3	1	4	2	3	1	3
	Nurturant	4	2	3	5	4	5	2
	Pro-social	5	3	5	3	6	6	5
	Aggressive	6	6	6	6	5	4	6

Median Rho between all pairs = +.54

There is less uniformity across cultures for peers as targets. In this case there is but one perfect correlation, that between Taira and Khalapur. The median value for Rho in this case is +.66, and only five of the fifteen comparisons are statistically significant. However, there are no negative values, the lowest being +.43, between Juxtlahuaca and Orchard Town.

Parents as targets show the least comparability in discriminative power across cultures, but even in this case, although some of the values were very low—+.09 for Taira and Tarong, Taira and Orchard Town, and Khalapur and Nyansongo—none of them were negative. The median value for Rho was +.54, and only three of the fifteen comparisons were statistically significant.

It seems to us that the similarity of the effect of these target types across cultures is remarkable. That infants would tend to evoke nurturant behavior in all cultures is not surprising. It is not unlikely that there is an instinctive base for this response; but, if not, cultures to be viable must see to it that the younger generations learns to help and support infants. Size alone explains why children are seldom aggressive toward their parents. If parental authority is added as a universal cultural role requirement it is even more understandable. We could go over the whole list and make similar post hoc sense of the findings, but it is improbable that we could predict the exact rank order for each of the three targets that was shown to be so similar across cultures.

Before accepting these effects, some questions of validity should be considered. To what extent is the similarity of rank orders across cultures true of the way in which the children really behaved rather than the result of judgment error? Such error may have been made either by the observer or by the coder. If it is assumed that both the observers and the coders made the implicit assumption that children were "naturally" nurturant to infants and dependent upon adults this may well have influenced their interpretation of acts with ambiguous content. Ambiguous acts to infants would have been classified as nurturant rather than dependent. Conversely, the same or a similar ambiguous act directed to a parent would be classified as dependent rather than nurturant. If this is true, the agreement that we were able to achieve between coders reflects merely that they had a common theory about the effects of targets upon social behavior. D'Andrade (1965) has illustrated this effect very cogently. He showed that convergence based on ratings does not necessarily mirror the external world. Although we do not believe that the uniformity of target effects across cultures is entirely due to coding bias, we believe that it has some effect.

GENERALIZATION ACROSS TARGETS

Can the clusters of social behavior under consideration be considered traits that generalize across situations or are they entirely situationally determined? Can it be said that there are nurturant or dependent or aggressive children in the sense that they will have a relatively high score on this trait to more than one target? Is there any evidence that the children of our sample had social personalities?

The evidence presented so far suggests that social behavior may be so bound by prescriptive and proscriptive rules that the occurrence of general "personality traits" seems unlikely.

The above problem can be explored using the same behavior clusters and targets as in the foregoing section. Whereas in that section we were concerned with discovering differences between pairs of targets, in this section we are concerned with similarities in the profile of a child's behavior across targets. This can be done by correlating the scores of each child on the behavior clusters across pairs of targets. We know from the preceding section that, on the average, 21 percent of a child's aggressive behavior is to infants and 24 percent to peers. If the same children who were above the mean on aggressive behavior toward infants were also above the mean on aggressive behavior toward peers, the correlation will be positive. If some children were aggressive only to infants, and others to peers alone, the value of the correlation would be negative. Positive correlations would support the trait theory, whereas negative correlations would not.

It may seem intuitively probable that pairs of targets that had the greatest discriminative power for a given behavior cluster could not have a high positive correlation in the present test of generalization. Such is not the case. The two tests are mathematically independent and empirically unrelated for this set of data (Rho = -.16).

The discriminative power of targets did, however, place one constraint upon our test of trait generalization. The inhibiting power of certain targets for certain of the behavior clusters resulted in such a skewed distribution of scores that a correlation was of dubious value. Such was the case for intimate-dependent and dominant-dependent behavior toward infants and aggressive behavior toward parents. As Figure 18 shows, the mean proportion scores were all under 5 percent. This indicates that most of the children had scores of zero. Correlations with such "top of the iceberg" effects have been indicated by brackets in Table 32. The Rho values were in fact low and represent three of the four negative correlations.

The remaining tests tend to support the hypothesis that there are indeed traits of social behavior that generalize across targets. All save one of the correlations are positive, and half of them (six of twelve) reach an acceptable level of statistical significance. Even including the dubious ones, the means of the tests for the three pairs are positive for each cluster.

This amount of generalization of social behavior across targets is similar, according to Mischel (1968), to what has been found in previous studies—generally positive but weak and variable correlations. Whether this supports a personality trait theory or a situational determinance theory depends upon one's expectations. As Burton (1963) points out, the consistency coefficients of +.30 to +.40 reported by Hartshorne and May (1928) in their famous study of honesty have been taken as evidence both for and against the hypothesis that this type of behavior is a generalized personality trait.

Whatever the merits of the consistency—specificity debate, the fact that we found generalization of behavior across targets has a bearing on the interpretation of the possible coding bias already discussed. If the status of the target of an act was—in the coder's mind—a part of the definition of all acts, and if each act was target-specific, there would of course be no generalization. This seems most likely to have occurred in nurturance to infants and in aggressive and intimate-dependent behavior to parents. Table 32 makes it clear that for nurturance the generalization from infants is low: r = +.11 to peers and +.04 to parents. The generalization of aggression from parents to other targets is negative to peers (–.10) and negligible to infants (+.04). Dominant-dependence does not generalize from parents to infants (–.01), but it does from parents to peers (+.35, P < .001). From this evidence it seems quite probable that our coders unconsciously took account of targets in deciding how to classify these three target-specific acts. It is less likely that the coders would have been so influenced for acts that are not target-specific, and show

Table 32. Correlations (Pearson r) for the scores of the pooled sample of children between pairs of targets.

Behavior cluster	Infant vs. peer	Peer vs. parent	Infant vs. parent	Mean
Pro-social	.31**[a]	.24*	.32**	.29
Sociable	.37***	.10	.03	.17
Nurturant	.11	−.01	.04	.05
Aggressive	.21*	[−.02]	[.06]	.08
Dominant-dependent	[−.05][b]	.35***	[−.01]	.10
Intimate-dependent	[.14]	.11	[.16]	.14

[a]Significance levels are indicated as follows: $P < .05*, < .01**, < .001***$.
[b]Brackets indicate that the correlation was based on mean scores of less than .05.

reasonably strong tendencies to generalize across targets. But the uniformity in ranks of behavior to targets across cultures shown in Table 31 should be somewhat discounted.

8   Regression Analysis

"Various positions have been taken as to the major determinants of a child's behavior. Gesell and Piaget, taking a developmental point of view, say the most important thing to know to predict a child's behavior is how old he is; Freud and his followers would insist that the most important determinant of a child's behavior is his life history, particularly his relationship with his father and mother; the learning theorists would insist that a knowledge of previous rewards and punishments for the particular behavior in question is what must be known. The Gestalt school, as exemplified by Lewin, Baldwin, and Barker and Wright, would take an ahistorical approach and insist that a knowledge of the situation, that is, the setting and the instigation, is the thing to know; and of course, the anthropologists would insist that if you don't know what society the child is a member of, you can't predict a thing. We suspect there is a grain of truth in each of these positions. In fact, we would add one more factor as possibly having some weight, that is, whether the child is a male or female." (Whiting, 1958.)

The results presented in this book suggest that indeed there may be some truth in all these positions. However, the analyses reported have not systematically considered the effects of interaction and redundancy among the sets of independent variables: culture type, sex, age, and target status. For example, the frequent assignment of the task of baby-tending to children in the simpler cultures was offered as one explanation for their high score on the nurturant-responsible end of Dimension A, and taken as proof of the influence of culture. It has also been shown that children, when interacting with infants, were most likely to be nurturant and least likely to be dependent; this was considered proof of the influence of situational factors. Are these two findings redundant? In this chapter we will check our data for redundancies and present the joint effects of the independent variables.

A multiple regression analysis was chosen* to explore the joint effects of culture type, sex, and age, and the status of infants, peers, and parents upon the six behavior clusters used as dependent variables in the last two chapters. Proportion scores, standardized over the whole sample to permit differences due to culture, were used in this analysis. Each independent variable was dichotomized, and the results presented in Table 33.

When the effects of status of the actor (sex and age) and of the target (infant, peers, and parents) are partialed out, culture still has a strong effect upon children's social behavior. Although the dependent variables used in the regression analysis were the six clusters rather

*In the program used (Data Text) variables are selected for a step-wise solution according to the highest partial correlation between the independent and dependent variables, controlling for independent variables already entered into the equation. Independent variables are entered step-by-step until the next independent variable adds less than .01 to the amount of variance accounted for as measured by R^2.

Table 33. Multiple regression of culture types, sex, age, and target type on six behavior clusters.

	Intimate-dependent (touches, seeks help)	Dominant-dependent (seeks dominance, seeks attention)	Nurturant (offers help, offers support)	Aggressive (assaults, insults, horseplay)	Pro-social (suggests responsibly, reprimands)	Sociable (acts responsibly, sociably)
1. Culture type						
Complex > simple	.17*[a]	.57***	-.30**	-.01	-.21*	-.07
Nuclear > non-nuclear		.15	-.13	-.17*	-.48***	.47***
2. Status of actor						
Girls > boys	.12	-.14	.20**	-.25**	-.05	.14
7-11-year-olds > 3-6-year-olds			.16*	-.22**	.32***	
3. Status of target						
Infant above $\bar{X}$ > below $\bar{X}$		-.08	.28**			-.31**
Peer above $\bar{X}$ > below $\bar{X}$	-.10			.25**	.16	-.23**
Parent above $\bar{X}$ > below $\bar{X}$	.43***	-.13	-.09	-.16		.06
R^2	.27	.38	.35	.23	.32	.30

[a] The numbers in each cell represent the standardized coefficient (Beta weight) for each independent variable at the last step of the regression. Empty cells indicate that a variable accounted for less than 1 percent of the variance for that behavior cluster. Significance levels are indicated as follows: $P < .05$*, $< .01$**, $< .001$***.

than the two dimensions previously used for estimating the effect of culture, it is evident that the contrast between children of complex and simple cultures shown in Table 33 is similar to that reported in Chapter 4. Children from complex cultures are more dominant-dependent and less nurturant than children from simpler cultures. Since these two clusters were at either pole of Dimension A, the results of the two analyses are similar. The fact that children from complex cultures are also more intimate-dependent and less pro-social differs from the findings given in Chapter 4.

The regressed effect of being a member of a culture favoring nuclear rather than non-nuclear households is also similar but not identical. Table 33 shows that nuclear cultures are high on the sociable and low on the aggressive and pro-social clusters. As can be seen, most of the behaviors included in these clusters were those of Dimension B, and the direction of association is similar. Differences are primarily due to minor variations in the way the component behaviors were clustered in the two analyses.

The effect of sex is also similar to that previously reported. Girls are more nurturant and boys more aggressive in both analyses. The direction of association by sex for both the intimate-dependent and dominant-dependent behaviors is also similar for the two analyses; the regressed scores do not control a significant amount of the variance. This corresponds to findings in Chapter 6 where the differences in these two behavior clusters were significant only at the younger age for the intimate behavior cluster and at the older age for the dominant-dependent cluster.

In both analyses the pro-social cluster increases significantly with age. The regressed scores for the nurturant cluster also increase significantly with age. They did so for girls only in the previous analysis. There are, however, two striking differences. First, age does not affect intimate-dependent behavior when the effects of culture, sex, and target are partialed out. In the previous analysis, this type of behavior decreased with age, especially for girls. The other striking difference is that there is a significant decrease with age for aggression in the regression analysis, whereas there was no apparent change with age for this cluster variable in the earlier analysis.

The regression analysis shows the greatest effect with regard to targets. In Chapter 7 behavior clusters showed significantly different mean proportions between most pairs of targets. When the influence of the other independent variables is partialed out, only five of the eighteen comparisons are statistically significant (see Table 33). Parents evoke intimate-dependent behavior, infants nurturant behavior, and peers aggressive behavior. Since the relation of sociable behavior is negative to both infants and peers, it is evident that parents evoke this type of behavior as well as intimate dependency. Targets have no significant regressed effect on the two remaining clusters: dominant-dependent and pro-social.

Thus culture type, the status of the actor, and the status of the target each affect one or another of the behavior clusters when the effects of the other two have been partialed out. The amount of variance controlled differs for each cluster.

A consideration of Table 33 by column rather than by row indicates that a different combination of independent variables is the best predictor for each behavior cluster. The significant predictors for the intimate-dependent cluster are parents as targets and membership in a complex culture. For the dominant-dependent cluster the only significant predictor is cultural complexity; for the nurturant cluster there are four—a simple culture, girls, older children,

168

and infant targets. Aggressive behavior is significantly predicted by
non-nuclear cultural membership, boys, and by being older; pro-
social behavior by simple and by non-nuclear cultural membership,
by being a boy, and by being younger. Finally, sociable behavior
is best predicted by a combination of belonging to a nuclear culture
and interacting with someone other than infants or peers.

The amount of variance controlled by the three sets of predictors
varies from an R^2 value of .23 for the aggressive cluster to .38 for the
dominant-dependent cluster. This range is quite respectable for a
nonexperimental study and we can say with some confidence that
there is some truth in the assumption that culture, sex, and situation
all contribute to the determination of the social behavior of children.

9   Conclusions

Since social behavior is intentional, we assumed that a set of motives or aims commonly characterizing the social acts of the children of the cultures studied would provide a basis of comparison. Notwithstanding the style used, children of all six cultures sought to help or to hurt one another, engaged in friendly exchanges or attempted to dominate, asked for help, called for attention, reprimanded or made responsible suggestions to one another. Although languages differed, certain features of the mode of social action were similar across cultures: the intent to injure could be accomplished by physical assault or verbal or gestural insult; intimacy could be manifested by a symbolic exchange or physical contact.

That only twelve categories were chosen was not completely arbitrary. Any social act to be successful must be understood. Actor and target must agree upon intent or the interaction goes awry. Social behavior is limited not so much by the capacity of the actor to vary his or her performance as by the audience's ability to interpret its meaning correctly. For this reason, as in other domains, the basic operational taxonomy is limited. In most cultures about a dozen basic kin terms suffice to refer to relatives representing an almost infinite number of degrees and types of relationship.

The infinite variety of speech sounds that a human is capable of making are reduced to between twenty and forty phonemes in most cultures. Most cultures have six or less primary terms for colors and not more than eleven. (Berlin and Kay, 1969). The number of distinctive features used to construct these taxonomies are limited in number and most are used in all cultures. No kinship system fails to use distinctions based on sex, age, generation, and parentage. Distinction in the point and mode of articulation are present in all phonemic systems, and the basic color terms of any culture refer to differences in brightness, hue, and intensity. Although individuals can and do make many more distinctions in these domains it is evident that the need for agreement between two people puts a severe limitation on the size and complexity of any taxonomy used in general social interaction.

It is not surprising that a limited number of categories was enough to describe the social behavior of the children of all six cultures. Furthermore, these categories were based on a limited number of features: the beneficiary of the transaction—ego, alter, or group; the nature of the goods or services involved in the transaction—help, support, dominance, or injury; and the mode of the transaction—physical or symbolic. This set of 3 × 5 × 2 distinctions yields a taxonomy with thirty primary categories if all distinctions are made.

Figure 19 is a paradigm of the types of behavior defined by the features that distinguish them. It can be seen that the reductions of the thirty primary categories to twelve results from merging and omission. Two categories were merged when the observers and/or

Goods and services	Mode	Ego	Alter	Group
Support Attention	Physical		Offers help	
	Symbolic	Seeks help		
	Physical	Seeks attention	Offers support	
	Symbolic			
Intimacy	Physical	Touches	////////	
	Symbolic	Acts sociably		
Dominance	Physical	Assaults sociably	////////	
	Symbolic	Seeks dominance	Suggests responsibly	
Injury	Physical	Assaults	////////	
	Symbolic	Insults	Reprimands	

Figure 19. A paradigm of the types of social behavior used in this study.

the coders could not or did not distinguish between the alter and the group for *offers help, offers support, suggests responsibly*, and *reprimands*. It was difficult to tell whether the actor or the target was the primary beneficiary of physical contact. No distinction at all could be made as to the primary beneficiary of *acts sociably*. Most omissions for categories involving the physical mode were made because the category never occurred or occurred so rarely that it was omitted.

As Nerlove and Romney (1967) pointed out in their cross-cultural study of sibling terminology, a domain with only eight primary categories yields over four thousand paradigms if all possible combinations are considered. Despite this, only eighteen were reported and 90 percent of the cases could be described by six paradigms. Arrangements that were cognitively disjunctive did not occur. If all the boundaries separating the thirty primary categories of social behavior suggested here could be either maintained or ignored, an astronomical number of variations would be possible for Figure 19. If the same set of distinctive features were used, paradigms most valuable in describing the children of other samples of cultures probably would differ somewhat from the one we have used, but we believe that, as was the case with sibling terms, a limited number is cognitively economical and the one used to describe the children of our study will be useful for other samples as well.

Even though the social behavior of children may be described in the twelve conceptually distinct categories mentioned, the frequency of the co-occurrence of various pairs over the six cultures was by no means random. When a correlation was run over the six cultures using median scores, the resulting matrix showed that many of the twelve behavior types were correlated strongly enough, either positively or negatively, to indicate that it would be unwarranted to treat each type separately. Such a procedure would have yielded results that, although appearing to be independent, were actually redundant. To simplify matters and reduce redundancy a scaling procedure (MDSAL) was applied to the matrix. This procedure yielded two interpretable dimensions.

The two dimensions yielded two scores that were calculated for each child in the sample by algebraically summing the behavior types that had the highest positive or negative values on each dimension. The score on Dimension A, arbitrarily labeled *nurturant-responsible versus dependent-dominant*, consisted of (*offers help* plus *offers support* plus *suggests responsibly*) minus (*seeks help* plus *seeks attention* plus *seeks dominance*). The score for Dimension B, *sociable-intimate versus authoritarian-aggressive*, consisted of (*acts sociably* plus *assaults sociably* plus *touches*) minus (*reprimands* plus *assaults*). These scores were the basis for investigating the effect of culture on the social behavior of children.

Two views are currently held concerning the comparison of children of different cultures. One emphasizes that because all children are human, the same developmental processes and sequences apply to children of all cultures. According to this assumption, although there may be differences in the rate of development from culture to culture or even the stage of development finally attained, such differences, if they occur at all, are of minor importance. The opposing view is that culture has such a profound effect that developmental sequences from one culture to another cannot be compared. Applied to the social behavior of children, the first point of view would predict little or no difference in the distribution of the scores of children from different cultures, whereas the second hypothesis would predict that the distribution of scores of the children of each culture would differ from every other.

Our results indicate that both these positions, taken in the extreme, are false, but that there is some truth in each. The results of this study indicate that cultures may be grouped in such a way that children brought up in one type behave in a similar, on the average indistinguishable, way from one another, but that children from contrasting types have score distributions that differ significantly. Specifically, based on the average score of their children on each dimension the six cultures fell into four types: Juxtlahuaca and Tarong, whose children had a positive average score on both dimensions; Khalapur and Taira, whose children had average scores that fell on the negative side of both dimensions; Nyansongo, whose children had average scores that fell on the positive side of Dimension A and on the negative side of Dimension B; and Orchard Town, whose children had average scores that fell on the negative side of Dimension A and the positive side of Dimension B.

Considering each dimension separately, Nyansongo, Juxlahuaca, and Tarong, with positive average scores on Dimension A, had children who were more nurturant-responsible and less dependent-dominant than the children of Taira, Khalapur, and Orchard Town. Grouped by Dimension B, the children of Juxlahuaca, Tarong, and Orchard Town were on the average more sociable-intimate and less authoritarian-aggressive than those of Taira, Khalapur, and Nyansongo. Thus, the children of the six cultures are neither all the same in their social behavior nor all different.

The results of our study also indicate that certain distinctions in the socioeconomic and domestic structures—the living arrangements, the daily routines, and the roles assigned to children in the six cultures—correspond and, presumably, account for the typology based on the children's social behavior.

The complexity of the socioeconomic system was a cultural feature that distinguished the cultures falling either high or low on Dimension A. Nyansongo, Juxlahuaca, and Tarong, whose children scores high on nurturant-responsible and low on dependent-dominant, had a relatively simple socioeconomic structure with little or no occupational specialization, a localized kin-based political structure, no professional priesthood, and no class or caste system. The settlement pattern consisted of dwellings with few or no public buildings.

Women in these cultures, being important contributors to the subsistence base of the family, had a heavy and responsible workload. The children in these cultures were expected to help their parents by doing economic chores and caring for younger siblings.

Khalapur and Orchard Town, the cultures whose children had relatively high scores on egoism and low scores on nurturance, had a more complex socioeconomic system characterized by occupational specialization, a central government, a priesthood, social stratification, and nucleated villages with public buildings. Women by and large depended on their husbands for economic support and did not contribute to food production. It was important for Orchard Town children to do well in school. For the Khalapur child who was enrolled in school, education was seen as an entry into a specialized cash earning job.

Most of the above features characterize Taira, whose children were also more dependent-dominant than nurturant-responsible. Occupational specialization was, however, not so highly developed, a priesthood was lacking, their social class system was incipient, and Tairan women were more heavily involved in food production than those of Khalapur and Orchard Town. Taira must be considered a borderline case on the scale of complexity.

Variations in household structure distinguish the two types of cultures whose children differed on Dimension B. Orchard Town, whose children scored high on the sociable-intimate side and low on the authoritarian-aggressive side, had a domestic structure based upon the independent nuclear family. Nuclear households were preferred and residence rules were flexible. The husband and wife usually ate together and slept together. The husband helped with the children and seldom physically assaulted his wife.

Nyansongo and Khalapur, whose children scored high on the authoritarian-aggressive side and low on the sociable-intimate side of Dimension B, had a domestic structure based on the patrilineal extended family. Residence rules were prescriptively patrilocal. Either patrilocal, lineal, or extended family households or mother-child polygynous households were preferred. Husbands and wives usually ate at separate times and in separate places and seldom slept in the same bed. Husbands were not permitted to be present at childbirth and were not expected to help care for infants; wife-beating was permitted.

Taira, also on the negative side of Dimension B, is again somewhat exceptional. Families of oldest sons had a patrilineal extended family with prescriptive rules of patrilocal residence and thus were similar to Khalapur and Nyansongo. Younger sons, however, usually established independent nuclear families more like those of Orchard Town, Juxtlahuaca, and Tarong.

It is our hypothesis that the clustering of most of the items by culture type in these six societies is not accidental but the result of the operation of general psycho-cultural principles. We believe that similar clusters of traits would be found in a wider sample of cultures. Some light could be thrown on this hypothesis by a cross-cultural investigation based on ethnographic evidence, but this is beyond the scope of the present study. A few comments are, however, appropriate. A number of cross-cultural studies (for example, Carneiro, 1970; Murdock, 1973) have shown that occupational specialization, a centralized political structure, social stratification, and a priesthood cluster in much the same way that they did in this study, and that these variables form a cross-cultural scale of cultural complexity. The economic role of women, however, does not appear as an item on this scale. A woman's participation in food production depends more upon the pattern of subsistence. Hunting and herding are usually carried out by men, while gathering and horticulture are most frequently women's work. Plow agriculture is male, wet rice both male and female. These economic features are more important than complexity in determining a woman's role.

It is not surprising that the social behavior of the children of each culture type usually was compatible with adult role requirements. Offering help and support is required of adults living in simpler societies, where the meeting of kin-based obligations and reciprocity with neighbors is essential; boasting and egoistic dominance are out of place there. In more complex communities, where relatives and neighbors are seen as competitors rather than persons to be helped and supported, boasting and egoistic dominance are often more appropriate responses than offering help and support.

The head of a corporated patrilineal extended family must be able to exercise authority over his adult sons and their families. To do this he must not be timid about expressing aggression, and the skill learnt in reprimanding younger siblings during childhood will stand him in good stead. The conflicting interests of three generations makes informal and intimate relationships difficult, particularly if all live in one household. The independent nuclear family, in which a husband and wife live together with their children, requires a much less authoritarian structure; an intimate and casual relationship is expressed by parents sleeping and eating together without other adults at the table or in the bedroom.

Formulas for appropriate adult social behavior dictated by the socioeconomic and family structures are imbedded in the value system of the culture. Nurturance and responsibility, success, authority, and casual intimacy are types of behavior that are differentially preferred by different cultures. These values are apparently transmitted to the child before the age of six. The younger children of our sample were already behaving in accordance with the expectations of their culture type. Our research was not focused on the details of the process by which these values were transmitted. The setting sampling procedures adopted resulted in too few observations of interactions between a child and his or her socializing agents to give an accurate account of intrinsic and extrinsic rewards and punishment, modeling, and identification, but some comments can be made with respect to each of these processes.

[handwritten margin note: These values are apparently transmitted to the child before age of 6.]

The influence of intrinsic rewards is most clearly evident in shaping a child's social behavior on Dimension A. Interaction with infants was shown at the cultural and individual level to induce nurturance and inhibit dependent-dominance. Probably because it reminds a child of his or her own expressions, it is distasteful to hear an infant cry and pleasurable to hear it laugh and see it smile. Furthermore, a child nurse who neglects or abuses a charge in the pursuit of his or her own pleasure ends up with a crying baby. Thus, giving help and comfort to infants is intrinsically reinforcing. Children charged with the care of infants will no doubt be punished by their parents if they are neglectful and irresponsible, but it is difficult to determine the relative importance of such extrinsic reinforcements in the development of nurturance.

The performance of economic tasks and domestic chores that contribute to family welfare are also intrinsically rewarding. A child does not have to be praised to experience pleasure from building a fire, cooking a meal, taking cattle to pasture and bringing them back, or gaining new knowledge from school. The more routine tasks such as washing dishes, sweeping the floor, or fetching wood are rote and perhaps less intrinsically rewarding.

The intrinsic rewards of task performance spring not only from the feeling of competence but from identification with parents. Children, envious of the privileges of adult status, feel a sense of satisfaction and pleasure in gardening if that is an important part of their mothers' role or herding if that is what their fathers do. Having been assigned a task, children are motivated to imitate the behavior of those who are competent. Their skills are more likely to come from observation then from instruction.

It should not be assumed that parents play an entirely passive role in the socialization process. It is in the assignment of tasks and the punishment of disobedience rather than in either deliberate instruction or rewarding and punishing specific behaviors that they have the greatest effect. This is borne out by the fact that most of the acts in which mothers were observed initiating interaction with children consisted of giving commands and making responsible suggestions. When questioned about consistency in obedience training, mothers in cultures where many domestic tasks were assigned were found to be more consistent than mothers in cultures where few such tasks were assigned. This suggests that parental reinforcements were directed more toward failure to carry out orders than toward errors of performance. In any case, our evidence suggests that whether a child is told to take care of younger siblings or is sent to school has a more profound effect upon the profile of the child's social behavior than the manipulation of reinforcement schedules by the parents.

Not all tasks assigned to children have the same effect on their social behavior. Tasks clearly contributing to the welfare of the family generalize to the nurturant side of Dimension A; those emphasizing individual achievement, such as doing well in school, have the opposite effect.

Identification and role imitation probably play an even more important part in shaping a child's behavior on Dimension B than on Dimension A. The formal, sometimes hostile, relation between a child's father and mother, the conflict between mother and grandmother or co-mother, and the authoritarian role of the grandfather provide quite a different set of adult models to a child brought up in an extended family than one brought up in the informal intimacy of a nuclear family. That the intrinsic reinforcement from interaction with parental targets plays a more important role than extrinsic reinforcements from parents is indicated by evidence from the mother interviews. When asked what they did when their children were aggressive toward them or fought with peers, mothers of children who scored on the aggressive side of Dimension B said that they were strict and punitive, while mothers of children on the intimate side of the dimension tended to be more permissive. If it can be assumed that the mothers of aggressive children actually were more punitive, and not just saying so, this was apparently not very effective. Some force greater than fear of their mothers' displeasure must have induced the children to be aggressive.

Originally we had hoped to discover whether variables had the same effects within and across cultures. Our data did not permit an adequate test of this important hypothesis.

Although distinct differences in the social behavior of children produced by the type of culture in which they grow up are apparent, there are striking uniformities across all cultures that can be accounted for by age and sex. To explore these, the two dimensions used for cultural comparisons were replaced by a set of six clusters combining

those behavior types that showed similar patterns of change by sex
and age.

As evidenced by sex differences, at the 3–5 age period both boys
and girls have different "childish" styles of social behavior. Boys engage in more horseplay, rough and tumble physical contact; girls
seek help or touch others more frequently. These behaviors decrease
sharply with age. Acting sociably, as coded, is another form of
"childish" behavior on which both young boys and girls score high,
but which also decreases with age. Boys remain more aggressive in the
older age group, insulting and continuing horseplay, and they increase
in seeking attention and dominance.

Sex distinctions also appear in "adult role" behavior. Boys and girls
are equally nurturant during the 3–5 age period, but the proportion of
nurturant behavior exhibited by girls increases rapidly as they grow
older, while the nurturant scores for the boys remain relatively
constant. Suggesting responsibly and reprimanding are not sex-typed;
they start low and increase rapidly with age for both boys and girls.

These effects of sex and age hold not only for the pooled sample
but with few exceptions for each of the six individual cultures. That
there are transcultural uniformities in the way that social behavior
changes with age is not surprising. It parallels well-known changes in
cognitive development during this period found to be similar in many
different cultures. The consistency of sex differences are perhaps
more surprising. Most interesting are rough and tumble horseplay and
intimate-dependency, which are significantly different during the 3–5
age period but not at older ages. Innate factors may play a part in
these differences. Sex differences that increase with age are more
likely to be culturally determined, and their similarity can be attributed to similarities in the roles of men and women in the six cultures.

Because we observed children in natural settings in which they interacted with a variety of people of different age, sex, and kin relation we were able to investigate the effect of the status of the target upon social behavior. Our scores—the same behavior clusters used for the inquiry into the effects of sex and age—showed that the children of our sample behaved quite differently to infants, peers, and parents. This was not unexpected. For effective social interaction every culture must have rules governing what behavior is appropriate and what is inappropriate for different diads. It was, however, surprising that the rank order of the six behavior clusters to the same target was remarkably similar across all cultures. In fact, such uniformity made us wonder whether it was not partly due to unconscious coder bias. A child showing off (seeking attention) to an infant might be judged as being nurturant (offering support), while the same act directed toward a peer might be classed in the dominant-dependent rather than the nurturant cluster. If the status of the target was the sole determinant for classifying social behavior, the observed rank order similarity across cultures should be attributed to the minds of the coders rather than to the real world. Our evidence indicates that, whereas this might partially explain the high proportion of nurturance to infants and dependence to parents, it cannot account for those behavior clusters for which the status of the target shows little discriminative power. Nor can it account for the observed generalization across targets. We therefore believe that, despite coding bias, infants, peers, and parents have discriminative power to evoke or inhibit certain responses that are common to children both within and across cultures.

The generalization of behavior across targets also sheds some light on the question of whether "personality traits" exist or whether all behavior is controlled by situation. Even though the status of targets (the situational factor) was a powerful determining influence on children's behavior, there was generalization across targets (the personality factor). Thus, children who were above the median of the whole sample on sociability to peers were also above the median in sociability to infants. Although this tendency for behavior to generalize across targets was evidenced by positive correlations, the values were low. Pro-social behavior alone showed a strong and significant tendency to generalize across all targets. Since this cluster increased significantly with age, the findings may indicate that older children can be expected to practice their newly acquired knowledge of the rules of the culture by making responsible suggestions or reprimanding anyone who deviates from these rules. By contrast, younger children tend not be behave this way to anyone. Thus our findings suggest that, throughout the world, two of the dominant personality traits of children between seven and eleven are self-righteousness and bossiness.

The question of interaction and redundancy between various sets of independent variables was explored in a regression analysis. Although some redundancy was discovered, each set of independent variables—culture type, sex, and age, and the status of the target—all had robust effects even after interactive effects had been partialed out. Some clusters were most strongly effected by culture type, others by sex and age, still others by the status of the target. Not one of the three sets of variables showed a clear preeminence in controlling children's social behavior.

Above all, the findings of this study suggest that none of the traditional theories alone can account for the social behavior of children. That boys are more aggressive and less nurturant than girls cannot be completely explained by either a biological or a cultural model. The children of each culture are unique in some respects but indistinguishable in others. Differences in learning environments produce differences in children's social behavior; despite this all children seek help and attention from adults and offer help and support to infants.

Appendix A. Examples of Twelve Summary Act Categories

01 _Offers help_

This category includes behavior interpreted by the rater as attempts on P's part to help O. It includes the offering of or giving of food or objects, when the rater judged either that O wanted the offered object or that P intended to help O. This type of behavior is defined in the field guide as nurturance: "In the presence of knowledge that someone else is in a state of need or drive, nurturance consists of tendencies to try to alleviate this state in the other person" (Whiting et al., 1963, p. 10).

def. of nurturance

Examples.

Little girl cries for a kamachili and reaches for it. Alfonso says, "No, No. _I'll give it to you,_" _and puts the piece in her mouth._

Edita is eating. Her baby sister wanders over to her and _Edita hands her a kamachili, saying, "here, here."_

Ana puts her foot in Edita's lap and points to something. [It is probably an insect bite.] _Edita looks at it, then scratches it._

When Ana complains that hers is "small, small," in a tone of great disappointment, *Edita gives hers to her.*

02 *Suggests responsibly*

This category includes suggestions on the part of P which he is judged to make because he is being responsible—that is, playing the adult role—or suggestions on P's part which try to make O do something P thinks that O, as a responsible person, should do.

Examples.

Justina tells Rosita [2-year-old sister] *to take cloth to the kitchen and give it to Andrea.*

Keiko says, *"Give a little* [berries] *to Suzoko"* [year-old baby on Hiroko's back].

Kazuyori calls over to Kiroko [sister, 8 years] *to take the baby.*

Brigida says, *"There in front"* [i.e., there are more desks to move down in the front of the classroom]. *"We'll bring it down together."*

03 *Reprimands*

P points out that O has broken a rule. This includes reprimands, warns, threatens, and accuses of deviation, which are defined as follows:

1. Reprimands: any verbal or physical punishment by one with authority to issue it. Authority may be derived from formal status relationship or from reference to rules generally recognized by the group, e.g., rules of the game or of the family or community.

Examples

Atsuo eats some fruit. Osamu [a toddler] tries to get some; *Atsuo says, "no, stop."*

Ombasa is working in the garden. Younger brother is playing with a stick, pretending to dig but not paying attention to the small plants. Ombasa calls, "Oh, you're digging in the garden—*stop!*"

2. Warns. Threatens natural consequences or alerts.
  Example.
Girl is walking on road carrying thatch on her head. Elizabeth, seeing a bus approaching, calls out, *"Get away, a bus is coming!"*

3. Threatens (in the role of a caretaker).
  Example.
Manyara should be taking a nap, but tries to get up. Rebecca: *My mother's coming to kill you if you don't go to sleep.*

4. Accuses of deviation. Include in this category cases where P accuses O of deviating.
  Example.
Ricardo: I've been stuck by thorns. Crescencio: *Why did you bring this kind* [tool]—*they can stick you?* Ricardo: You were the one who told me to.

04 *Seeks dominance*

P attempts to subordinate O by suggesting what O should do. This includes commands and directions given by P to O which are not judged to be attempts to help or reprimand O and are not given by P in his role as a caretaker or responsible person—i.e., do not fall in types 1, 2, or 3. It excludes suggestions which seem to be made primarily for the purpose of initiating a friendly interaction.

Examples.

Edita to sister, *"Go get the ball."*

Shirley to girl next to her, *"Move over."*

05 *Acts sociably*

Behavior which is friendly (affiliative) and which appears to be instrumental in establishing friendly interaction. It includes making suggestions or behaving in other ways judged to be intended to initiate friendly interaction. It includes greeting behavior. It should be scored when P joins a group to participate in a game or some other activity, but not used if protocol starts with statement that P is playing with children.

Examples.

Ombasa is on the path between her mother's house and the co-wife's house with baby brother. Nyanchama: *Look for the kitten and we'll tie him up.*

Agnes is sitting holding baby brother *talking to Obebo.* We follow them into the pasture. *Ogaro greets us.*

Zosima comes out of the house and stands with a crowd of visiting girls her own age and older. No interaction for awhile. *Zosima grabs Edita's hands laughing, both laughing.*

06 *Seeks attention*

Include behavior on the part of P which is intended to catch the attention of O when the desire seems to be to get praise or a positive response from O. Include clowning behavior and bragging.

Examples.

Romulo's mother just told a child that she would give him a sweet
if he would allow her to cut his nails. *Romulo* [urgently] *"umm-
umm"* (to call attention to self).

David raises his hand in the classroom.

*Jim runs off, putting bag over himself, swinging it, trying to get
attention by screaming and running around.*

Alberto, holding up a blob of mud he has been toiling over, pro-
claims proudly, *"Mine is just like a chair!"*

Pedro and sister are playing game, P: Now you spin. *Ha, ha, I'll win.*

Barbara to observer: *I have a pad that's way bigger than that one!*

Taurino stands up and says, "Look, here is a big rock." *José stands
up also, puts his hands in his pockets, and begins to jump
between the rocks from side to side. He cries, "Taurino, Taurino,
see how I am jumping."*

07 Offers support

Include in this category behavior where P praises or encourages O.
Include smiling at individuals if the intent seems to be to offer
emotional support or encouragement. Include behavior intended to
distract O when sad and make him smile or express pleasure.

Examples.

*Jeanne jumps up and down with the rest of her team and shouts
"Yea!" as her team wins.*

*Rebecca picks up the crying baby, kissing it, singing to it, jouncing
it up and down, singing songs and making the baby dance as she
held it.*

Yasuo turns to Masaru, "Masaru bring milk to us." Masaru goes around pouring milk. He comes over to Yasuo. As Masaru pours milk, Yasuo says: *"He is good to us, don't you think so?"*

Suddenly there is a fight between Kembo and his little brother. Masuru just sits on the concrete in the same position and watches them. *Then he eggs Kembo on: "Gouge out his eyes, gouge them out."* [Kembo successfully fights his brother until the smaller one screams, Kembo chasing after him.]

Petro watches Ogoi [older brother, aged 6] play with cigarette package. *Petro smiles when Ogoi gets it apart.*

Joseph's brother is fighting and playing lightheartedly with a friend. *Throughout, Joseph is watching them closely, laughing and smiling but not participating.*

08 Touches

Behavior on part of P which indicates desire for physical contact with O when the intent is judged not to be aggressive as it would be in horseplay and roughhousing.

Examples.

Joseph places his elbow on Pedro's shoulder.

Pacifico leans on Brigida's lap.

Elizabeth has pushed Agnes off her lap and tells her to take a hoe into the house. Agnes refuses, and *keeps coming back to lie on Elizabeth's lap.*

A herd of goats and cows come down the road, fairly quickly. Ogoi sits up, comments on the noise of the goat bells, then leans over against the older boy. As the goats pass *he puts his hand on the leg of the older boy.*

The two children are crowded together on one chair, Rosalina with her arm around Antonia, while they watch their aunt prepare tortillas.

09 Seeks help

This type of behavior includes asking for something for the benefit of the speaker (P). It may be a verbal or gestural request for help, and includes requests for food or possessions.

Examples.
Girls are straightening the classroom. *Brigida calls "Help me too."* [wants help moving desk]
Trying to undo sack and failing, Kheer passes it to another boy and says, *"try to open this."*
Samiko to mother: *I'd like some food.*
Ombasa asks friend to help her tie the baby on her back.

10 Assaults sociably (horseplay)

This category includes hitting, shoving, kicking, striking with a stick or other object, wrestling, etc., when the rater judges that it was done in the context of play or in a playful way and seems to be within the rules of the game or within the accepted definition of playful.

Examples.
Edita grins, *slaps the other girl on the elbow,* then runs laughing as the girl jumps and turns around.
Edita playfully tries to pinch Anita's ear.
Romulo and friend *wrestle; both laugh.*

193

11 Assaults

The same type of behavior as assaults sociably when it is judged that P is doing it with the sole purpose of hurting O.

Examples.

A boy starts to walk by. *David pushes him back.*
Petro throws a stone and hits his cousin on the chest.

12 Symbolic aggression

This category includes insulting, threatening by gesture or by verbal statement, challenging, frightening, chasing, taking or attempting to take property against the desire of O, and destroying or attempting to destroy property. Again acts that are instrumental to affiliation —i.e., playing or interacting playfully with O—should be distinguished from those acts which seem to be done with the sole intent of hurting O. Distinguish verbal behavior in this category from reprimanding and dominating: 03 and 04. Reprimands are made in the context of being responsible. Dominance is done with the idea of changing O's behavior, but is not intended to hurt or to symbolically hurt in the process of playing.

Examples.
Insults Playfully
Kheer [giggling] to Rampaal: *You're a big old man!* Rampaal: No, I'm not. Why do you call me an old man? Kheer: *You're an old man and big.* Rampaal hits Kheer, then runs away.
Edita stands and laughs at the other girl who cannot quite get the desk into place.

Justina and Zosima are sucking candy. They are quiet for a few moments, wandering around near the door, sucking their candies noisily. *Zosima suddenly turns to Justina and does a combination raspberry and spit in her face.* They both shriek and giggle.

Insults

Masaru walks back to the table; girls follow too. Masaru shouts at them "get away, get out of here!" Kuniko answers, "Masaru, you crooked head!" *Masaru makes a face at her.*

Frightens playfully

Brigida grabs Asuzena's hand laughing and they have a little tug of war, both laughing. Asuzena pulls free of Brigida, who bends toward her and says laughingly, *"I'll give you to him"* [meaning observer].

Angel is playing with his siblings and cousins. They are playing with masks, one of which is from the dance of the devils. Angel puts the mask over his face, holding it up with one hand. *He runs toward his sister through the street laughing and crying "look at the devil."*

Gitoi and Manyara are playing with calabashes in the door of the house. Lawrence walks up to the house from a nearby pasture where he is herding cattle. Manyara, seeing Lawrence, says to Gitoi, *"You're going to be taken."*

Threatens

Yokiko comes walking up from behind him. *Fukataro turns around and raises his stick menacingly.*

Takes property playfully

Clarita and Justina are playing tug of war with a banana peel.

Clarita pulls and gets the peel. Justina slaps the peel from Clarita's hand; the two scramble for it, giggling. *Clarita gets the peel,* both still giggling.

Challenges

Jane holds out piece of paper just out of reach of Martha. Martha: I can get that. *Jane: Try it!*

Rebecca comes out, chasing Joseph, yelling as she runs after him, then turns around and runs away so Joseph can chase her.

Chasing, shoving, and so on

In swimming contest David shoves someone in the water.

Appendix B. Code for Behavior Observations

Column

1 *Deck* 4, 5 (double punch)

2 *Society*
   0. N.A.
   1. Okinawa
   2. Philippines
   3. India
   4. Mexico
   5. New England
   6. Africa

3 *Class of P*
   0. N.A.
   1. Younger boy, 3–6
   2. Older boy, 7–10
   3. Younger girl, 3–6
   4. Older girl, 7–10
   5. Other

Column

4 *P's identity*
   1–6.

5 *P's age*
   0. N.A.
   1. 3
   2–8. 4 . . . 10
   9. Over 10

6 *Size of group*
   0. N.A.
   1. P alone
   2. P + 1
   3–8. P + 2 . . . 7
   9. P + 8 or more

Column

7 *Setting: authority*
   0.   N.A.
   1.   Authority present
   2.   Authority absent

8 *Setting: activity*
   0.   N.A. or other
   1.   Play
   2.   Casual social inter-
       action
   3.   Work
   4.   Learning

9 *Setting: place*
   0.   N.A.
   1.   Play area
   2.   Work area
   3.   School
   4.   Home
   5.   Other's house
   6.   Sacred place

10 *Sex of instigator*
   0.   N.A.
   1.   P
   2.   Male
   3.   Female
   4.   Males
   5.   Females

Column

10 *Sex of instigator* (cont.)
   6.   Mixed
   7.   Animal
   8.   Inanimate object

11 *Age grade of instigator*
   0.   N.A.
   1.   P
   2.   Infant (0–3)
   3.   Younger child (3–6)
   4.   Older child (7–10)
   5.   Adolescent (10–18)
   6.   Adult
   7.   Children
   8.   Mixed; adults and
       children

12 *Relation of O to P: age*
   0.   N.A.
   1.   P
   2.   Younger
   3.   Same age
   4.   Older
   5.   Group, P included
   6.   Group, P excluded

13 *Relation of O to P: kin*
   0.   N.A.
   1.   P

Column

13   *Relation of O to P: kin* (cont.)
- 2.   Sibling
- 3.   Parent
- 4.   Grandparent
- 5.   Uncle, aunt (or others in same household)
- 6.   Other
- 7.   Teacher
- 8.   Investigator, observer
- 9.   Group
- X.   Co-wife or co-husband
- Y.   Co-grandparent

14–

15   *Instigating act*
- 00.   No instigation or N.A.
- 01.   Punished physically
- 02.   Withholds reward
- 03.   Miscellaneous reward
- 04.   Miscellaneous punishment
- 05.   Isolates: threatens to send away
- 06.   Frightens: threatens

Column

15   *Instigating act* (cont.)
-      action by supernatural
- 07.   Teaches
- 08.   Reprimands: negative suggestion after the fact
- 09.   Warns: threatens natural consequence of act
- 10.   Assaults on person
- 11.   Insults
- 12.   Threatens physically by gesture
- 13.   Threatens punishment by speaker
- 14.   Takes property against desire of possessor
- 15.   Destroys property
- 16.   Accuses of deviation
- 17.   Reports deviation
- 20.   Suggests
- 21.   Arrogates self
- 22.   Challenges to competition
- 23.   Refuses to comply

Column

15 *Instigating act* (cont.)
- 24. Is self-reliant
- 25. Blocks
- 26. Accepts challenge
- 30. Gives up set
- 31. Complies
- 32. Deprecates self
- 33. Hides
- 34. Avoids
- 35. Acts shy
- 40. Encounters difficulty
- 41. Hurts self
- 42. Acts hurt
- 43. Asks for help (includes food or object, if obviously succorant)
- 45. Seeks approval
- 46. Seeks physical contact
- 48. Asks permission
- 50. Gives help (includes giving food or object, if obviously nurturant)
- 51. Gives emotional support or affection

Column

15 *Instigating act* (cont.)
- 52. Gives information
- 53. Gives approval
- 54. Gives permission
- 60. Joins group interaction
- 61. Greets
- 62. Observes, listens
- 63. Shows pleasure
- 64. Starts group game
- 65. Is sociable (initiates friendly interaction, etc.)
- 70. Deviates
- 71. Has unsharable object
- 72. Is tempted
- 73. Admits guilt
- 74. Denies guilt
- 75. Makes amends
- 76. Apologizes
- 77. Resists temptation
- 80. Adults working
- 82. Adults interacting
- 83. Mother or adult nurtures sibling
- 84. Children working

Column

15 *Instigating act* (cont.)
- 85. Children playing
- 86. Children fighting
- 87. Encounters danger
- 89. Encounters something requiring responsible action
- 90. Ignores
- 91. Breaks interaction
- 92. Solitary play
- 93. Practices skill
- 94. Is responsible
- 96. Solitary work

16 *Purposive nature of act*
- 0. Not indicated
- 1. Accidental
- 2. Instrumental
- 3. Imitative
- 4. Goal
- 5. Adult role
- 6. Instrumental, retaliatory
- 7. Instrumental, adult role
- 8. Instrumental, imitative

Column

17 *Behavior system adverbs: positive*
- 0. N.A.
- 1. Aggressively
- 2. Submissively
- 3. Nurturantly
- 4. Sociably
- 5. Responsibly
- 6. Achievemently
- 7. Self-reliantly
- 8. Dominantly
- 9. Succorantly

18 *Miscellaneous adverbs*
- 0. N.A.
- 1. Guiltily
- 2. Justifyingly
- 3. Self-consciously
- 4. Excitedly
- 5. Irresponsibly, carelessly
- 6. Slowly
- 7. Sadly
- 8. Happily
- 9. Other

19 *Intensity*
- 0. N.A.

Column

19   *Intensity* (cont.)
1.   +, action repeated or strongly
2.   –, weakly
3.   Parallel action of O and P (the instigator is P; the instigation is 00; and 3 equals the intensity after the central act, i.e. Column 24).

20–

21   *P's response* (same as Column 14–15)

22   *Purposive nature of act* (same as Column 16)

23   *Behavior system adverbs: Positive* (same as Column 17)

24   *Miscellaneous adverbs* (same as Column 18)

25   *Intensity* (same as Column 19)

Column

26   *Obedience-compliance*
0.   N.A.
1.   Complies
2.   Does not comply

27   *Sex of object* (same as Column 10)

28   *Age grade of object* (same as Column 11)

29   *Relation of object of P's response to P: age* (same as Column 12)

30   *Relation of object of P's response to P: kin* (same as Column 13)

31   *Relation of object of P's response to instigator*
0.   N.A.
1.   Same
2.   Different

32   *Sex of agent* (same as Column 10)

33   *Age grade of agent* (same as Column 11)

Column

34   *Relation of agent to P: age*
     (same as Column 12)

35   *Relation of agent to P: kin*
     (same as Column 13)

36–

37   *Effect act* (same as Column
     14–15)

38   *Purposive nature of act*
     (same as Column 16)

39   *Behavior system adverbs:*
     positive (same as Column 17)

40   *Intensity* (same as Column
     19)

41   *Obedience-compliance* (same
     as Column 26)

Column

42–

43   *Protocol number*
     00.   N.A.
     01.   Protocol #1
     02.   Protocol #2

44–

45   *Act number*
     00.   N.A.
     01.   First act
     02.–49   Second act, etc.
             (acts within stan-
             dard 5-minute
             period)
     50–99   (acts not within
             standard 5-minute
             period)

Appendix C. Samples of Five-Minute Observations

[handwritten annotation: They illustrate the variation in style and detail of recording]

(These observations have been randomly selected. They illustrate the variation in style and in detail of recording.)

NYANSONGO

Child observed: Ogoi, 4-year-old boy
Date: 1 February 1957 *Time:* 1:45 P.M.
Place: A pasture
Present: Lawrence, Ogoi's 6-year-old brother
Aloyse, 6-year-old boy
Peter, 8-year-old boy
Manyara, 11-year-old boy

Peter, Aloyse, Lawrence, and Manyara are sitting together. Ogoi is standing on the edge of the group, holding Manyara's slingshot. He comes over to the group and sits down with them. Manyara grabs the slingshot from Ogoi, who makes no protest at all. Manyara is snapping the rubber of the slingshot against Aloyse's foot, with the latter's permission. Everyone, including Ogoi, is intently watching and laughing when Aloyse gets hit. Then Manyara stops. Aloyse spits on Ogoi. Ogoi angrily whines, "Don't spit on me like that." Lawrence tells Aloyse, "You wipe that off him." Aloyse ignores him.

Lawrence says to Ogoi, "Go get the cows." Ogoi does. Peter and Aloyse go to retrieve their own cows. Ogoi is higher up on the hill but runs down to where Lawrence and Manyara, who have moved with the other boys, are. Ogoi sits down with them. Lawrence asks him, "What's in your mouth?" Ogoi opens his mouth to show. Peter, who has just come over, says, "Open your mouth and let's see." Ogoi smiles and opens his mouth. They all tell him to stick out his tongue. He does and all peer in. Suddenly there is fighting between Peter and Manyara. Ogoi just sits and watches it for a long time. Lawrence playfully grabs at Ogoi's foot. He laughs. Lawrence pushes Ogoi over on his back. Ogoi smiles. Lawrence, looking into Ogoi's mouth, says, "Oh look! Here's a tooth that's going to come out!" Ogoi is still smiling as Lawrence pushes him around on the ground some more. Lawrence and Ogoi then go and join the group which is now shouting across to the next hill that their cows have gone into the maize field. They continue shouting for about five minutes.

Child observed: Rebecca, 5-year-old girl
Date: 1 February 1957 *Time:* 3:05 P.M.
Place: A field
Present: Moriasi, Rebecca's baby brother
Mokeira, 4-year-old girl cousin
Nyaberi, 7-year-old boy cousin
Kengaya, Rebecca's aunt

Rebecca is hoeing with Kengaya. Mokeira, Nyaberi, and Moriasi
are also there. Interrupting her hoeing, Rebecca suddenly goes to pick
up her baby brother. She jounces him around a lot, and he cries.
"Why do you cry now?" she asks, "I've nothing to give you." She
slaps him on the head and pushes him hard. He cries. Rebecca then
puts him on her back.

Mokeira goes into a little nearby house and shouts, "Rebecca, I've
got my hoe!" "No, that's mine. Don't touch it," Rebecca replies. She
carries Moriasi over to another baby, who is in front of a bigger
house, and says to the second baby, "Can't you walk to your mother?" She lifts up this baby, kissing it, singing to it, jouncing it up
and down, and making it dance as she holds it.

Mokeira starts wrestling with Rebecca. Rebecca continues wrestling and laughing, and while doing so moves quite a far distance
away from the babies. The aunt sees this retreat and says to the girls,
"Why are you leaving babies here?" Rebecca immediately comes
running back and proceeds to amuse the babies by singing and danc-
ing.

Mokeira calls to Rebecca from afar, "Hey, come here. Let's go this
way." Rebecca goes off with her, but soon returns to the babies.
She then starts tussling with Nyaberi. He has taken a pencil from her,
and she chases him about trying to retrieve it. Again, Mokeira calls,
this time from the other hut. Rebecca goes to her and asks, "Why did
you call me?" Mokeira has something to show her and says, "See
these things." Rebecca looks briefly, then runs back to the babies.

JUXTLAHUACA

Child observed: Teresa, 8-year-old girl
Date: 21 April 1956 *Time:* 1:07 P.M.

Place: At home in the cookshack
Present: Lola, Teresa's mother
       Cirilo, Teresa's 4-year-old brother

Lola is seated on the ground cleaning dried chilies. Cirilo is seated between Lola and the door; Teresa is standing by him. Lola says to Teresa, "Give me the bowl." Teresa walks over to where the pots and kitchen utensils are kept, pulls out a large spoon, and gives it to her mother. "The bowl," says Lola. Teresa leaves the spoon on the floor and walks over again and gets the bowl. She wipes it off and hands it to Lola who dips into the chilies with it.

Teresa goes to a basket, pulls out a piece of tortilla, and goes out into the patio with it. She sits down on a log and begins to eat, looking into the cookshack. Almost without transition, she stands up again, enters the cookshack, and sits down next to Lola who is seated by the fire.

Lola takes a branch of herb from the wall and cuts off a piece, throwing it into the broth. She says to Teresa, "Take a piece of this herb to your grandmother." Teresa stands up, breaks off a small branch, and goes into the patio. She calls toward the other house, "Grandmother, did you find your herb?" The grandmother apparently answers that she has it. Teresa returns and puts the herb back with the rest.

Lola places the chilies on the grinding stone and begins to grind them. Looking at them, she says to Teresa, who has remained standing next to the wall with her arms hanging down, "Give me the large spoon." Teresa bends over, picks up the spoon from the ground where she had left it before and puts it in Lola's hand. Lola takes the spoon and washes it.

Teresa moves away from her mother, sits down on a bag, and combs her hair by running the fingers of both hands through it.

Cirilo goes out to the patio and returns with a box of matches. The matchbox is empty. He stops in the doorway. Teresa goes over to him and says, "Give me your matches." She tries to take the box away from him by force, but is unable to do so. Teresa says, "Don't eat the match. You'll die and they'll bury you with your violin like they do in Copala." Lola laughs and tells the observer that it is the custom in Copala to play the violin at burials. Teresa continues to try to get the box of matches from Cirilo, but he holds it tightly and cries, "Mama!" Lola, not looking at them, says "Umm."

Teresa says to Cirilo, "Get that guitar of mine." He stands up and digs into a basket, pulling out a small toy guitar. Teresa comes over to him and tries to take it away from him forcibly. Cirilo moves away from her with a quick movement, lifts the guitar over his head as if to hit her with it, but hits the air. He throws the guitar down on the floor. Teresa throws herself on top of him and the two roll on the floor, Teresa laughing gaily, but Cirilo very serious.

Teresa stands up and remains looking at Cirilo. He picks up a dirty piece of watermelon from the floor, a part of the rind that has already been eaten, and begins to bite into it. Lola raises her gaze and asks, "What are you eating?" Cirilo doesn't answer, but Teresa says, "He's eating matches." Cirilo then says, "No, I'm breaking up my watermelon." He puts the piece of watermelon on the guitar and begins to move the piece of watermelon about to make noise.

Teresa draws away from Cirilo, sits down on a bag, and again combs her hair with her hands.

Lola asks, "Aren't you going to eat, Lilo [nickname for Cirilo]?" Lola continues, "I'm going out." Teresa says, looking at the floor,

"Mama's going out." Cirilo looks at Teresa, leaving the guitar on the floor, and says, "Aren't you going to eat?" Teresa answers, "I'm going to eat as soon as mother leaves."

Cirilo takes the guitar and begins to hit the floor with it very hard. Teresa says, "Stop, stop, you are going to break it." Teresa goes out into the patio. From there she looks back into the cookshack and says to Cirilo, "Stop that. You're going to break it." Cirilo is still banging the guitar on the floor. Lola looks at him and says, "What's the matter, don't you hear? Stop that, you are going to break it."

Child observed: Mariano, 6-year-old boy
Date: 12 July 1956 *Time:* 5:27 P.M.
Place: Street in front of Mariano's gate
Present: Mariano's 2-year-old brother
          Three town boys

Mariano and three older boys are playing. Mariano's younger brother is close by, but is not part of the group. As the boys run back and forth across the street, the youngster follows but is always far behind. As the younger brother reaches the middle of the street, he falls down (trips on a rock). Burros are being driven rather slowly down the street. The 2-year-old rolls over on his stomach, fairly close to the side of the street, but does not stand up; the burros come closer and he gives a frightened cry, but not too loudly. An older boy turns to Mariano and says, "Get your brother, the burros are coming!" Mariano turns and looks toward the brother and then quickly runs around the front of the group to his brother. By this time the burros have walked on by and the brother has stopped his outcry, but is hiccuping slightly. Mariano picks his brother up, stands him on his feet, and brushes the dirt off his shirt. He puts the sombrero back on his brother's head and straightens it without speaking. Mariano then takes his brother's hand and leads him out of the street, over to the wall. There they stand together looking out at the street but not touching hands. The older boys turn and go off down the street. Mariano looks after them as they go, then starts off also, one step. He hesitates, looks back at his brother, and calls, "Come." Mariano waits and the brother starts coming slowly. Mariano returns, takes his brother by the hand, and pulls him along a step or two. By this time the older boys are out of sight. Mariano drops his brother's hand, turns, and goes back down the street to his own gate. He starts inside, pushing the heavy gate open a couple of inches more. Then he turns and goes back to his younger brother, who is standing where Mariano left him. Mariano takes his hand and leads him through the gate. Inside, Mariano walks over to where his mother is grinding in the shade of the house in the patio. He pushes his brother forward before the mother, then steps back, turns, and starts away. Another boy, different from the others but not Mixtecan, is standing in the doorway. Mariano says, "I'm going to play," and runs over to the boy. They stand at the corner of the house and push at each other gently with hands against hands. Then both boys go into the street and play with a piece of rope. It is tied to one boy as if a horse, while the other holds the rope in his hand like the driver, but both boys run side by side not one ahead of the other.

TARONG

Child observed: Crescencio, 7-year-old boy
Date: 27 July 1955 *Time:* 5:52 P.M.

Place: At home with visitors present for a party
Present: Josefa, Crescencio's mother
          Felisa, Crescencio's 16-year-old sister
          Loreto, Crescencio's 3-year-old sister
          Pacífico, Crescencio's 8-month-old brother
          Estafina, Crescencio's aunt
          Agueda, Crescencio's aunt
          Simeon, 6-year-old boy cousin
          Adriano, 3-year-old boy cousin
          Andrés, baby boy cousin
          Mario, baby boy cousin

Everyone is seated in the sala (living-room) and adjoining porch. Crescencio is seated on the floor trying to amuse a tired and fussy Pico (nickname for Pacífico).

Crescencio stands, wanders to a corner of the room, and looks for a tin can or something to amuse Pacífico. Pico, wailing loudly by now, crawls to Josefa. She picks him up and rocks him a little in her arms; but Pico continues to wail and looks sleepy and cross. Josefa calls to Crescencio, "Here, put him to sleep." Crescencio smiles, crosses the room to Josefa, and takes the baby. He turns and goes toward the weaving room. As he goes, Estafina calls after him, "La, you put him to sleep." Crescencio goes into the weaving room, to a hammock hung there. Felisa comes in after Crescencio; Crescencio lays the baby in the hammock. She says, "Do it this way," then returns to the sala. Crescencio stands, rocks the hammock by its ropes, and sings to Pacifico, who is quieter but still fussing occasionally.

Josefa, grinning widely and conspiratorially, crosses the room and sits just next to the door to the weaving room, where she can hear well but Crescencio cannot see her. Meanwhile, Pacífico's fusses grow into a wail. Crescencio rocks violently and sings louder; he makes soothing noises and then sings more. Adriano goes into the weaving room. Crescencio and Adriano mutter together a moment, then Crescencio sits in the hammock, cuddles Pacífico, holds him closely, and coos at him. Adriano pushes the hammock the way one pushes a swing, as he and Crescencio start to sing loudly.

Josefa, in the sala, is now peeping through the door crack, convulsed with silent laughter. Estafina crosses the room and squats next to Josefa to peer also. Simeon, followed by Mario, wanders into the weaving room where he stands watching the performance critically, though laughing.

Adriano dashes out of the room, through the sala, and out onto the porch. Still sitting next to him in the hammock, Crescencio lays Pico down and pats him. Simeon pushes the hammock gently by the ropes and coos at Pico, who is having a fit by now. Crescencio picks him up, cuddles him, and rocks him in his arms. He says to Simeon, "Take Mario away; he is 'itchy-cooing' the baby. How can he sleep?" Simeon picks Mario up and goes out into the sala with him where he deposits the child with Felisa.

Crescencio calls "Simeon! Simeon!" Simeon goes back into the weaving room. Crescencio again lays Pico down and pats him. Simeon rocks the hammock as before. The baby fusses some but quiets down as Simeon rocks gently and Crescencio sings, coos, and pats Pico.

Child observed: Marina, 10-year-old girl
Date: 12 August 1955 *Time:* 3:50 P.M.
Place: Yard of house #7 in cluster of houses adjoining Marina's
Present: Leonida, Marina's infant sister

Gertrudes, Marina's 4-year-old sister
Perlita, Marina's 2-year-old sister
Puri, 12-year-old girl
Charles, observer's infant son
Dominga, 12-year-old girl
Corazóna, Dominga's 9-year-old sister
Andrés, Dominga's infant brother
Norma, 4-year-old girl
Large group of other children

Marina, holding Leonida, stands watching the younger children running about. She swings the baby up in front of her until their faces are level. Grinning at Leonida, she rubs noses with her.

Puri wanders past Marina, carrying Charles. As she passes, she leans over and makes noises ("Ba, ba, ba") at Leonida. Marina smiles at Puri.

Marina pulls a nursing bottle from her pocket and presents it to Leonida who seems interested. Dominga comes up and looks at the bottle. She says, referring to the nipple, "It looks like a breast." Marina smiles and rubs her hand through the baby's hair. Norma dashes past. In doing so she brushes against Marina who whirls around saying, "Heh?" She squats down, cradling the baby in her lap, and holds the bottle for her. Dominga crouches next to Marina and the two smile as they watch the younger children, encouraged by Puri, chasing each other in a circle. The baby stops eating and yawns. Dominga says, "Perhaps she is sleepy." Marina, tickling the baby's neck, replies, "She just woke up." Marina laughs as some of the running children collide and fall in a giggling heap. Dominga starts the game again. Marina watches Leonida who is playing with the nipple of her bottle and cooing. She stands, arches her back, and yawns again. Perlita wanders over and stands beside them.

Puri comes past with some flowers in her hand. Stopping in front of Perlita, Puri, smiling, holds out the flowers and asks, "Which is it like, sampaguita or rosal [two varieties of flowers]?" Marina smiles as Perlita looks "ashamed" and hangs her head. Marina says to Perlita, "Guita, you say sampaguita." She smiles at Puri, who grins back and then wanders off.

Marina, laughing, watches the children play. She moves across the yard toward Corazóne who is holding Andrés. Corazóne smiles at Leonida and asks, "She has teeth already?" Marina answers proudly, "Yes." Córazone asks, "How many?" Marina answers, "Two."

The game is now noisy and Marina watches it, laughing. Juggling Leonida, she says, "Hee, hee, hee" to her.

TAIRA

Child observed: Osamu, 5-year-old-boy
Date: 14 February 1955 *Time:* 2:15 P.M.
Place: Lane in front of a friend's house
Present: Hitoshi, 4-year-old-boy
Sumiko, Hitoshi's 10-year-old sister
Susumu, 4-year-old boy

Osamu and Hitoshi are playing with a large ball. Osamu throws the ball to Hitoshi, who misses it and has to run after it. Hitoshi retrieves the ball and aims it at Osamu, who is bent over with his hands on the ground in front of him. Laughing each time, Hitoshi hits Osamu's head with the ball three times. Osamu only laughs and remains in the bent-over position while Hitoshi hits him twice more. Then Osamu runs into the yard. Hitoshi continues to play with the ball. Osamu calls him from the yard but Hitoshi doesn't answer. Osamu calls again but Hitoshi still doesn't answer. Instead, Hitoshi walks over to Susumu, who has wandered by. Osamu asks Hitoshi to get the ball which he has thrown into the potato field across the yard. Hitoshi gets the ball but throws it in a direction away from Osamu. Osamu runs for the ball and Hitoshi runs after him. Osamu gets the ball and Hitoshi runs after him asking for it. Laughing gleefully and with the ball in his arms, Osamu runs from Hitoshi. He throws the ball and both chase it. They reach the ball at the same time, and Osamu accidentally pushes Hitoshi out of the way as he grabs for the ball. Hitoshi whines, "Beru! [I don't like it!]" Osamu plays with the ball. Hitoshi goes over to him, pushes him down, and sits on him. They struggle. Just as Hitoshi steps over Osamu, Sumiko, his older sister, calls out, "Dirty Hitoshi!" Hitoshi steps aside, and Osamu looks up, stands up, and walks over to the stone wall where he sits with the ball in his hands. He watches Susumu pounding with an iron piece on a rock. Hitoshi runs into the yard and disappears behind the house.

Child observed: Yuriko, 6-year-old girl
Date: 24 April 1955   *Time:*   4:10 P.M.
Place: In and around the village
Present: Kiyoko, Yuriko's infant sister
Kazufumi, 5-year-old boy

Yuriko, carrying Kiyoko on her back, walks around a banyan tree where a group of girls are playing. Although she is quiet, Yuriko lightly slaps the baby's behind to pacify her. The girls by the tree are all looking at a book, but Yuriko merely glances in their direction and continues to walk around. Kiyoko coughs a little, and Yuriko says, "Don't cry," and hops up and down in order to calm the infant. She walks back and forth with rapid steps. Again she glances at the girls who are reading.

As she walks up the road past the store, Yuriko hums to herself and taps the baby's behind again. On the way she meets Kazufumi, who also is carrying a baby on his back. His baby is crying. "Attend to the child," she shouts as they pass by. Kazufumi walks on, as does Yuriko without looking back.

She approaches the group of girls again but still does not join them. She restlessly continues to walk, singing to herself, and slapping the baby's bottom. She goes to her house and inside the yard, to the kitchen, then back to the yard.

KHALAPUR

Child observed: Dhyaan, 10-year-old boy
Date: 17 December 1954 *Time:* 8:10 A.M.
Place: The courtyard
Present: Dhyaan's mother
         Preem, 8-year-old boy cousin
         Dhyaan's 13-year-old sister
         Laksman, Dhyaan's older brother

Preem is rolling a hoop and Dhyaan, leaning on a cot, is watching him. Dhyaan goes toward the kitchen and says to his mother, "Today I will go early." (He means to the fields.) His mother is holding a dish of hot water and says to him, "*You* wash your hands in hot water." The mother sits down in the courtyard and starts washing her hands. Dhyaan goes into the kitchen where his older sister is at the cooking hearth. He says, "Give me some hot water." His sister says, "Get it yourself." Dhyaan shouts at her, "Don't be silly!" His sister hits him several times with a stick from the fire. He hits back at her. She hits him harder and then picks up the tongs and shakes them at him. Dhyaan picks up a wooden sandal and shakes it at his sister. Their mother shouts at them, "Aren't you ashamed of yourselves?" To her daughter she says, "Go and sit down and don't fight." Dhyaan puts on the sandals and goes back out into the courtyard.

Dhyaan stands behind his mother. Laksman brings his slate to the mother and washes it from her water. Dhyaan watches. The mother shouts at the older brother, "Go and get the water." She does not want him to wash with hers. The sister goes over to Dhyaan and says, "Give me my sandals." She takes them from him. "Take, take, take," says Dhyaan. Then he says, "Eeee, Ma! Ma, it's cold." The brother is just about finished washing his slate with the mother's water. Dhyaan says to him, "It is all right now. Go and put chalk on it."

Child observed: Kamlaa, 10-year-old girl
Date: 17 March 1955 *Time:* 11:05 A.M.
Place: Kamlaa's house
Present: Mrs. Makkhan, Kamlaa's grandmother
Nacklii, Kamlaa's year-old boy cousin
Mrs. Dhiaar, Kamlaa's aunt and Nacklii's mother
Mimlaa, 13-year-old girl

Mrs. Makkhan and Mrs. Dhiaar are cooking. Kamlaa comes back from seeing if Mimlaa is going to the fields. She wasn't able to find her because Mimlaa has just entered Kamlaa's courtyard. Kamlaa comes in after her and says, "I went to your house to see you and you weren't there." Mrs. Makkhan says to Kamlaa, "Now take this food to the fields." Kamlaa answers, "Let me eat mine first." Mrs. Makkhan says, "Take the food to the fields and eat yours there." Kamlaa replies, "No, I will eat here."

Nacklii has been inside sleeping. He wakes up and begins to cry. Kamlaa goes inside, gets him, and brings him back out saying, "No, I will eat here, because there won't be any left for me." Mrs. Dhiaar shouts, "Don't we give you any food?" Mrs. Makkhan says, "All right, we'll set your food aside for you." Kamlaa says, "All right." Mrs. Makkhan tells her, "Go quickly."

ORCHARD TOWN

Child observed: Tom, 4½-year-old-boy
Date: 25 January 1955 *Time:* 3:08 P.M.
Place: The kitchen, then a pond behind the house
Present: Jane, Tom's 6-year-old sister
Tom's mother
Judy, 6½-year-old girl
John, 4½-year-old boy

Tom and Jane are getting ready to go ice skating on a pond behind their house. Tom asks his mother to buckle his coat. His sister urges him to hurry. The mother says, "Now if you get cold you come back and let me put something on you. You want a scarf, Jane?" Jane says she doesn't and neither does Tom. The children pick up their skates and go outdoors. Both run down the yard and climb over the stone wall to the little pond. Tom runs over to Judy and says, "Oh, I didn't know you could ice skate." He then goes out on the ice and says, "This is too soft. John! Don't do that!" (John is stepping on the thin edges of the ice and breaking it.) Tom then says to John, "John, I bet you don't go to school yet." Tom sits down on a rock and starts putting on his skates. John says, "Yes, I do. I'm in the third grade." Tom says, "No, you're not," and John replies again that he is. Tom says to Judy, "Judy, you can't skate." Judy says, "Yes, I can." John asks Tom if his skates are his own, and Tom replies that they're Jane's. John then tells Tom that he's putting his skates on wrong, which Tom at first denies. After a pause Tom admits, "You're right, John. I got it in the wrong place." John tries to help him saying, "It goes right here." Tom says, "No! Don't!" Jane asks Tom if he can put his skates on by himself. Tom looks up laughing and says, "Yes. Sure. Mama says we have to get these on nice and tight."

Child observed: Virginia, 4-year-old girl
Date: 1 March 1955 *Time:* 2:46 P.M.
Place: The kitchen
Present: Jimmy, Virginia's 2-year-old brother
Virginia's mother

Virginia and Jimmy are playing policeman. Virginia is policeman and Jimmy is pushing a truck around. Virginia tells him when to stop and go. She says, "Jimmy, go get some Howdy Doody juice," then tells her mother, "Mama, I want some Howdy Doody juice." Her mother says, "Okay," and gets out some orange juice. Virginia screams, "No! I don't want that kinda juice!" Her mother asks, "Well, what kind do you want?" Virginia answers, "I want the Howdy Doody juice." Then she says, "Mama, give me that candle up there. I want the candle man." Her mother says, "Okay," but does nothing about it. Jimmy takes the juice from his mother and brings it to

Virginia who is sitting in a high-chair. Virginia takes it from him. Her mother tells Virginia to thank her brother. Instead, Virginia talks to her mother about her toy. Her mother replies, "Well, that figures, Virginia." Virginia laughs and says to her mother, "Oh, you always say that," and then to Jimmy, "Jimmy, did you say that? If you don't be good, I'll bring the garbage and I'll put it on your head." She laughs again and sits with a half-eaten apple in one hand and a glass of juice in the other. Jimmy finishes his juice. Virginia tells him to put his glass on the table. Jimmy says, "No." Virginia says, "Yes." The mother asks Jimmy to get Virginia's glass. Virginia says, "I'm not through." Jimmy goes over to Virginia and waits for her glass. Virginia hands him the glass and he brings it to his mother who says, "Thank you." Virginia says to Jimmy, "Jimmy, you shouldn't a-said thank you. I said you shouldn't a-said thank you." She gets off the chair and chases Jimmy around the house in a circle.

Bibliography

Barker, Roger G., and Herbert F. Wright. 1954. *Midwest and Its Children.* Evanston, Ill.: Row, Peterson.

Barry, Herbert, III, Margaret K. Bacon, and Irvin L. Child. 1957. A Cross-cultural survey of some sex differences in socialization. *Journal of Abnormal and Social Psychology* 55:327–332.

Barry, Herbert, III, Irvin L. Child, and Margaret K. Bacon. 1959. Relation of child training to subsistence economy. *American Anthropologist* 61:51–63.

Beller, E. K. 1959. Exploratory studies of dependency. *Transactions of the N.Y. Academy of Science* 21:414–426.

Benedict, Ruth. 1934. *Patterns of Culture.* Boston: Houghton Mifflin.

Berlin, Brent, and Paul Kay. 1969. *Basic Color Terms.* Berkeley: University of California Press.

Bronfenbrenner, Urie. 1958. Socialization and social class through time and space. In E. E. Maccoby et al., eds., *Readings in Social Psychology,* 3rd ed. New York: Henry Holt.

Bruner, J., R. Olver, and P. Greenfield. 1966. *Studies in Cognitive Growth.* New York: John Wiley and Sons.

Burton, Roger V. 1963. Generality of honesty reconsidered. *Psychological Review* 70 (6):481–499.

—— and J. W. M. Whiting. 1961. The absent father and cross-sex identity. *Merrill-Palmer Quarterly of Behavior and Development* 7:85–95.

221

Carnerio, R. L. 1970. Scale analysis, evolutionary sequences and the rating of cultures. In R. Naroll and R. Cohen, eds., *A Handbook of Method in Cultural Anthropology*. Garden City: Doubleday.

Child, Irvin L. 1954. Socialization. In G. Lindzey, ed., *Handbook of Social Psychology*, vol. II. Cambridge, Mass.: Addison-Wesley.

Cole, M., J. Gay, J. Glick, and D. Sharp. 1971. *The Cultural Context of Learning and Thinking*. New York: Basic Books.

D'Andrade, Roy G. 1965. Trait psychology and componential analysis. *American Anthropologist* 67:215:228.

Dasen, Pierre. 1972. Cross-cultural Piagetian research: A summary. *The Journal of Cross-Cultural Psychology* 3:23–39.

—— 1973. Concrete operational development in three cultures. Paper presented to the First Regional Conference in Africa. International Association for Cross-Cultural Psychology. Ibadan, Nigeria.

Dawson, J. L. M. 1967. Cultural and physiological influences upon spatial-perceptual process in West Africa. *Int. Journal of Psychology* 2:115–128; 171–185.

Dollard, John. 1953. *Steps in Psychotherapy*. New York: Macmillan.

DuBois, Cora. 1944. *The People of Alor: A Socio-psychological Study of an East Indian Island*. Minneapolis: University of Minnesota Press.

Edwards, Carolyn, 1972. Dependency as a system of behavior in children. Unpublished manuscript.

Ember, Carol. 1973. Female task assignment and the social behavior of boys. *Ethos* 1:424–439.

Erikson, Erik H. 1939. Observations of Sioux education. *Journal of Psychology*, 7:101–156.

—— 1950. *Childhood and Society*. New York: W. W. Norton.

Fischer, John L., and Ann Fischer. 1963. The New Englanders of Orchard Town, U.S.A., in B. Whiting, ed., *Six Cultures*. Vol. 5 of Six Culture Series.

Gewirtz, J. L. 1954. Three determinants of attention-seeking in young children. *Monographs of the Society for Research in Child Development* 19 (2) [Serial No. 59].

Gladwin, Thomas, and S. B. Sarason. 1953. *Truk: Man in Paradise:* New York: Viking Fund Publications in Anthropology, No. 20.

Goodnow, J. J. 1967. Problems in research on culture and thought. In D. Elkind and J. H. Flavell, eds., *Studies in Cognitive Development*. New York: Oxford University Press.

Hallowell, A. I. 1942. Acculturation processes and personality changes indicated by the Rorschach technique. *Rorschach Research Exchange* 6:42–50.

Hartshorne, H., and M. A. May. 1928. Studies in the nature of character. Vol. I: *Studies in Deceit*. New York: Macmillan.

Havighurst, R. J., and A. Davis. 1946. Social class and color differences in child-rearing. *American Sociological Review* 11:698–710.

Henry, W. 1956. The Thematic Aperception Technique in the study of group and cultural problems. In H. Anderson and G. Anderson, eds., *An Introduction to Projective Techniques*. Englewood Cliffs, N.J.: Prentice-Hall.

Hess, Robert D. 1970. Social class and ethnic influences on socialization. In P. H. Mussen, ed., *Carmichael's Manual of Child Psychology,* vol. II, 3rd ed. New York: John Wiley and Sons.

Hull, Clark L. 1943. *Principles of Behavior*. New York: Appleton-Century-Crofts.

Kagan, Jerome, and H. A. Moss. 1962. *Birth to Maturity*. New York: John Wiley and Sons.

Kaplan, Bert. 1961. Cross-cultural use of projective techniques. In F. L. K. Hsu, ed., *Psychological Anthropology*. Homewood, Ill.: Dorsey Press.

Kardiner, Abram, and Ralph Linton. 1939. *The Individual and His Society*. New York: Columbia University Press.

Kardiner, Abram, Ralph Linton, Cora Dubois, and James West. 1945. *The Psychological Frontiers of Society*. New York: Columbia University Press.

Koch, H. L. 1956. Attitudes of children toward their peers as related to certain characteristics of their siblings. *Psychologocal Monographs* 70:1–41.

Kohlberg, Lawrence. 1969. Stage and sequence: The cognitive developmental approach to socialization. In David Goslen, ed., *Handbook of Socialization Theory and Research*. Chicago: Rand McNally.

Kruskal, J. B. 1964. Multidimensional scaling by optimizing goodness of fit to a nonmetric hypothesis. *Psychometrika* 29:115–129.

Lambert, William, L. Minturn Triandis, and M. Wolf. 1958. Some correlates of beliefs in the malevolence and benevolence of supernatural beings: a cross-cultural study. *Journal of Abnormal and Social Psychology* 58:162–169.

LeVine, Robert. 1970. Cross-cultural study in child psychology. In P. H. Mussen, ed., *Carmichael's Manual of Child Psychology*, vol. II., 3rd ed. New York: John Wiley and Sons.

LeVine, Robert A., and Barbara LeVine [Lloyd]. 1963. Nyansongo: A Gusii community in Kenya, in B. Whiting, ed., *Six Cultures*. Vol. 2 in Six Cultures Series.

Longabaugh, Richard. 1963. A category system for coding interpersonal behavior as social exchange. *Sociometry* 26:319-344.

—— 1966. The structure of interpersonal behavior. *Sociometry* 29:441-460.

McClelland, D., and G. Friedman. 1952. A cross-cultural study of the relationship between child-training practices and achievement motivation appearing in folk tales. In G. Swanson, T. Newcomb, and E. Hartley, eds., *Reading in Social Psychology*. New York: Holt, Rinehart and Winston.

Maretzki, Thomas W., and Hatsumi Maretzki. 1963. Taira: An Okinawan village, in B. Whiting, ed., *Six Cultures*. Vol. 7 in Six Cultures Series.

Mead, Margaret. 1928. *Coming of Age in Samoa*. New York: William Morrow.

—— 1930. *Growing up in New Guinea*. New York: William Morrow.

—— 1935. *Sex and Temperament in Three Primitive Societies*. New York: William Morrow.

Miller, Neal E., and John Dollard. 1941. *Social Learning and Imitation*. New Haven: Yale University Press.

Minturn, Leigh, and William W. Lambert. 1964. *Mothers of Six Cultures: Antecedents of Child Rearing*. New York: John Wiley and Sons.

Minturn, Leigh, and John T. Hitchcock. 1963. The Rajputs of Khalapur, India, in B. Whiting, ed., *Six Cultures*. Vol. 3 in Six Culture Series.

Mischel, Walter. 1968. *Personality and Assessment*. New York: John Wiley and Sons.

Munroe, Robert L. and Ruth H. Munroe. 1971. Effect of environmental experience on spatial ability in an East African society. *Journal of Social Psychology* 83:14-22.

Murdock, George P., and Caterina Provost. 1973. Measurement of cultural complexity. *Ethnology* 12:379-392.

Murdock, George P., and J. W. M. Whiting. 1951. Cultural determinants of parental attitudes: The relationship between the social structure, particularly the family structure and parental behavior. In J. E. Senn, ed., *Problems of*

Infancy and Childhood. Transactions of the fourth conference. New York: Josiah Macy, Jr., Foundation.

Murray, Henry A. 1943. *Thematic Apperception Test Manual.* Cambridge, Mass.: Harvard University Press.

Nerlove, Sara. 1969. Trait disposition and situational determinants of behavior among Gusii children of Southwestern Kenya. Doctoral dissertation, Stanford University.

Nerlove, Sara, Ruth H. Munroe, and Robert L. Munroe. 1971. Effect of environmental experience on spatial ability: a replication. *Journal of Social Psychology* 84:3–10.

Nerlove, Sara, and A. Kimball Romney. 1967. Sibling terminology and cross-sex behavior. *American Anthropologist* 69:179–187.

Nydegger, William, and Corinne Nydegger. 1963. Tarong: An Ilocos barrio in the Philippines, in B. Whiting., ed., *Six Cultures.* Vol. 6 in Six Cultures Series.

Pavlov, I. P. 1927. *Conditioned Reflexes.* London: Oxford University Press.

Price-Williams, Douglass, William Gordon, and Manual Ramirez III. 1969. Skill and conservation: A study of pottery-making children. *Developmental Psychology* 1:769.

Romney, A. Kimball, and Romaine Romney. 1963. The Mixtecans of Juxtlahuaca, in B. Whiting, ed., *Six Cultures.* Vol. 4 in Six Cultures Series.

Sears, P. S. 1948. Measurement of dependency and aggression in doll play. *American Psychologist* 3:263.

Sears, R. R., J. W. M. Whiting, V. Nowlis, and P. S. Sears. 1953. Some child-rearing antecedents of aggression and dependency in young children. *Genetic Psychology Monographs* 47:135–234.

Sears, Robert R., Eleanor E. Maccoby, and Harry Levin. 1957. *Patterns of Child Rearing.* Evanston, Ill.: Row, Peterson.

Shweder, Richard A. 1973. The between and within of cross-cultural research. *Ethos* 1:531–545.

Skinner, B. F. 1953. *The Behavior of Organisms: An Experimental Analysis.* New York: Appleton-Century-Crofts.

Spindler, G. P. 1955. *Sociocultural and Psychological Processes in Menomine Acculturation.* Culture and Society Series, #5. Berkeley: University of California Press.

Super, Charles. 1970. Cognitive changes during the late pre-school years: Non-western evidence for universality. Paper presented at the Regional Meeting of the International Association for Cross-Cultural Psychology. Ibadan, Nigeria.

Swanson, Guy E. 1960. *The Birth of the Gods: The Origin of Primitive Beliefs.* Ann Arbor: University of Michigan Press.

Tatje, Terrence A., Raoul Naroll, and Robert B. Textor. 1970. The methodological findings of the cross-cultural summary. In R. Naroll and R. Cohen, eds., *A Handbook of Method in Cultural Anthropology.* Garden City: Doubleday.

Wallace, Anthony F. C. 1952. The modal personality structure of the Tuscarora Indians as revealed by the Rorschach Test. Bureau of American Ethnology, Bulletin #150. Washington, D.C.

White, S. H. 1968. Changes in learning processes in the late pre-school years. Paper presented at a meeting of the American Education Research Association, Chicago.

Whiting, Beatrice B. 1950. *Paiute Sorcery.* New York: Viking Fund.

——, ed. 1963. *Six Cultures: Studies of Child Rearing.* New York: John Wiley and Sons.

——. 1965. Sex identity conflict and physical violence: A comparative study. *American Anthropologist* 67:123–140.

—— and Carolyn Edwards. 1973. A cross-cultural analysis of sex differences in the behavior of children aged three through eleven. *Journal of Social Psychology* 91:171–188.

Whiting, J. W. M. 1941. *Becoming a Kwoma.* New Haven: Yale University Press.

——. 1958. The observation of children's behavior. Paper presented at the Annual Meetings of the American Anthropological Association.

——. 1960. Resource mediation and learning by identification. In Ira Iscoe and Harold Stevenson, eds., *Personality Development in Children.* Austin: University of Texas Press.

——. 1964. Effects of climate on certain cultural practices. In W. Goodenough, ed., *Explorations in Cultural Anthropology.* New York: McGraw-Hill.

——. 1973. A model for Psycho-Cultural Research. Distinguished lecture address delivered at the Annual Meetings of the American Anthropological Association, New Orleans.

Whiting, J. W. M., Eleanor H. Chasdi, Helen F. Antonovsky, and Barbara C. Ayres. 1966. The learning of values. In Evon Z. Vogt and Ethel M. Albert, eds.,

People of Rimrock: A Study of Values in Five Cultures. Cambridge, Mass.: Harvard University Press.

Whiting, J. W. M., and Irvin L. Child. 1953. *Child Training and Personality.* New Haven: Yale University Press.

Whiting, J. W. M., Irvin L. Child, William W. Lambert et al. 1966. *Field Guide for a Study of Socialization.* Six Cultures Series, vol. 1. New York: John Wiley and Sons. Reprinted by Krieger Publishing Co., Huntington, N.Y.

Whiting, J. W. M. et al. 1953. *Field Manual for the Cross-Cultural Study of Child Rearing.* New York: Social Science Research Council.

Whiting, J. W. M., and Beatrice B. Whiting. 1973. Altruistic and egoistic behavior in six cultures. In L. Nader and T. W. Maretzki, eds., *Cultural Illness and Health: Essays in Human Adaption.* Washington, D.C.: American Anthropological Association.

Zubin, J. 1954. Failure of the Rorschach technique. *Journal of Projective Techniques* 18:303–315.

Index

Abbott, Susan, 120n
Achievement, 40, 54, 63, 181
Adolescent, as target, 153
Adult: presence of at observations, 45; as target, 153. *See also* Grandparents, Parents
Adverbs, qualifiers in code, 54, 55
Agarie, Nariyuki, viii
Age: effect of, 1, 136–151, 167–168; of children in sample, 32; of mothers, 33; and likelihood of being home, 43–44; and child care, 132; effect of on sex differences, 139–145, 181–182; and sex differences, 145–151, 182; factor in regression analysis, 165–169
Age categories: for chores, 92, 94; for sex-age groups, 136–137; for sex differences, 145
Aggression, 40; punishment for, 10; opportunity vs. instrumental, 61; assaults, 61, 127; assaults socially, 57, 61, 127; insults, 61; attitudes of mothers toward, 108–110; between husbands and wives, 123; reprimands as, 127; changes in by age and sex, 142–144, 168; by

target type, 156; on regression analysis, 169
Agriculture: women's workload in, 83; child's share in, 92, 103. *See also* each village by name
Altman, Jean, ix
Animals, care of: children's role in, 89, 103; herding of, 90–92
Assaults sociably, 56, 57, 61
Authoritarian-aggressive polar cluster score, 70; children included in, 114; linked to extended families, 129
Ayres, Barbara, viiin

Bacon, Margaret K., 10, 144
Baldwin, Lawrence, x
Barker, Roger G., 5, 6, 40
Barrios, 15; in Juxtlahuaca, 24, 78
Barry, Herbert, III, 10, 144
Behavior: as index of personality, 5–6; restrictions on range of, 6; observation of, 39–42; recording, 40–42; coding of protocols for, 54; categories of, 56–63; innate, 149. *See also* Behavior categories; Social behavior

Index

Virilocal residence, 115; in Tarong, 116; in Juxtlahuaca, 116; in Taira, 116–117; in Khalapur, 117–119; in Nyansongo, 117–119

Wallace, Anthony F.C., 4
Water supplies, children's role in, 86–87, 88, 103
Weisman, Mark, ix
White, S.H., 142
Whiting, B., vii, viii, ix, 4, 9, 42, 67, 71, 144, 149

Whiting, J.W.M., viii, 5, 8, 9, 10, 67, 164
Wife-beating, 123, 176
Women, role of, 176, 178
Workload, mother's, 83, 130–131; rank order in Six Cultures, 110; and tasks delegated to children, 110–113; and socioeconomic structure, 176
Wright, Herbert F., 5, 6, 40

Yogi, Kiyoshi, viii

Zubin, J., 4